Tennessee
CURIOSITIES

Help Us Keep This Guide Up to Date

Every effort has been made by the author and editors to make this guide as accurate and useful as possible. However, many things can change after a guide is published—establishments close, phone numbers change, hiking trails are rerouted, facilities come under new management, etc.

We would love to hear from you concerning your experiences with this guide and how you feel it could be made better and be kept up to date. While we may not be able to respond to all comments and suggestions, we'll take them to heart and we'll also make certain to share them with the author. Please send your comments and suggestions to the following address:

Globe Pequot Press
Reader Response/Editorial Department
P.O. Box 480
Guilford, CT 06437

Or you may e-mail us at:
editorial@GlobePequot.com

Thanks for your input, and happy travels!

Curiosities Series

Tennessee CURIOSITIES

Quirky characters,
roadside oddities &
other offbeat stuff

Kristin Luna

Guilford, Connecticut

Copyright © 2011 by Morris Book Publishing, LLC

Photos by Kristin Luna unless otherwise noted.
Maps by Mary Ann Dube copyright © Morris Book Publishing, LLC
Text design: Bret Kerr
Layout artist: Casey Shain
Project editor: John Burbidge

Library of Congress Cataloging-in-Publication data

Luna, Kristin.
  Tennessee curiosities : quirky characters, roadside oddities & other offbeat stuff / Kristin Luna.
     p. cm.
  Includes index.
  ISBN 978-0-7627-5997-2
  1. Tennessee—Guidebooks. 2. Tennessee—Description and travel. 3. Curiosities and
wonders—Tennessee. 4. Tennessee—Miscellanea. I. Title.
  F434.3.L86 2011
  976.8—dc22
                              2010036738

Printed in the United States of America

10 9 8 7 6 5 4 3 2 1

For my parents, Jeanie and Greg Luna,
for raising me with such fine Southern values

Tennessee

contents

introduction

★ ★

*I*t took leaving Tennessee to realize what I had, what had always been there. As a native of a small rural town smack dab in the center of the state, I spent the first twenty-two years of my life trying to figure out how to get out. Now, I'm constantly searching for ways back in. After circling the globe a number of times, visiting nearly all of the fifty states, and having lived in multiple European countries, as well as the American Southwest, New England, and now the West Coast, I appreciate how truly unique my roots are.

Meat-and-threes, fried green tomatoes, biscuits with apple butter, fried pickles, and all things sweet potato, I'm not going to lie, I eat my way through the state—and, no coincidence, pack on the pounds while at it—every time I return home for a visit. I've yet to sample rooster fries, though, and as adventurous as I may be, I'm not quite sure I have it in me (you'll have to read the coming pages to find out what I'm referring to).

But who knew there was more to a state than merely its culinary offerings (the most important facet, if you ask me)? Turns out, my home has far more to boast about than deep-fried delicacies. Even having spent the majority of my life in the Volunteer State, I learned more than I ever could have imagined while researching this book. Who knew there was an elephant sanctuary a mere hour from my house, that women gaining the right to vote was largely due to Tennessee, that the state is home to a burgeoning pearl farm, and that so many historic figures continue to haunt every hole and holler this side of the Mississippi? I always knew I came from a special place, but writing this book shed new light on that fact and granted me a humbling dose of perspective.

I'm sure as the years pass, I'll continue to come across new curiosities that I'll wish I'd known about in time to include them here, but for now I just hope you enjoy reading about Tennessee's quirks as much as I did discovering them.

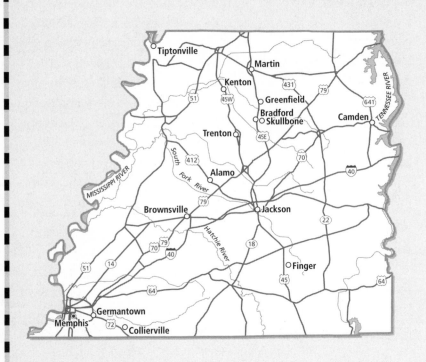

West Tennessee

1

West

The border of West Tennessee—one of the state's three grand divisions—is an anomaly in itself. Not straight, not jagged, it's bubble-shaped with curves and dips that are defined by the Mississippi River. The region's eastern border is made up of the Tennessee River, which grazes Alabama, Arkansas, Mississippi, Kentucky, and Missouri.

When driving along I-40, bisecting the state diagonally, you'll pass through stretches of barren wasteland—boondocks is an accurate word to describe it—though, like anywhere, you'll find hidden gems scattered haphazardly about. But then the West has its prized possession—Memphis—in the far most southwestern corner, which more than makes up for the rest.

Memphis has got soul, there's no denyin'. In fact, it would be hard to live in Tennessee's biggest city without a deep-burning love for all things musical. Everyone plays an instrument or backup sings in a band or spends his or her free nights after work hitting the live music joints on Beale. It's not just a passion, it's a way of life.

The obvious crooners—Elvis Presley, Johnny Cash, B. B. King—aside, Memphis has produced more than a few top acts. Justin Timberlake. Al Green. Otis Redding. Three 6 Mafia. From hip-hop to R & B, jazz to soul, there's musical flavor for the taking in this thriving hot spot.

Aside from being Tennessee's most soulful city, Memphis is also the most crowded—crowded by equine, that is: There are more horses per capita in Shelby County than in any other county in the United States.

★ ★

A Drive-Through Zoo
Alamo

Rural Tennessee, in the town of Alamo (population 2,400), might be the last place you'd expect to be off-roading when you just happen to stumble upon a rambunctious Bornean bearded pig rolling in the mud, with a couple of placid zebras grazing in the distance. Nevertheless, that's exactly what you'll find in this Crockett County seat. (Yes, as in Davy . . . and the Alamo . . . get the connection now?)

Ever since 1967—a hundred years after it began serving as an agricultural farm—Hillcrest Farm, which now houses Tennessee Safari Park, has been working on building its collection of game animals. The first inhabitants were a herd of buffalo that belonged to the state. Today, more than forty years later, the safari park features 300-plus animals representing sixty-three different species. Not too shabby for a town thousands of miles and an ocean away from Africa.

Alongside more typical animals like camels, swans, ostriches, warthogs, and kangaroos, you'll see gazelles, cranes, water buffalo, two-toed sloths, and much, much more. And the best part is you don't even have to observe from afar: You can drive through the park (by appointment only) and have the animals come right up to your vehicle.

Tennessee Safari Park is located at 637 Conley Rd. in Alamo. For more information, call (901) 734-6005 or visit www.tennessee safaripark.com.

Doodle Soup Capital of the World
Bradford

Yes, that is indeed a thing and a place. And the town that boasts such a claim, Bradford, even has a sign commemorating its lofty achievement. Doodle soup is a delicacy pretty much found only in these parts of Tennessee (if found elsewhere, I've yet to spot it on the menu). It consists of chicken, distilled red vinegar, salt, dry cayenne pepper, and a little bit of both flour and sugar. Like any good recipe, it's tweaked and altered depending on the chef, but that's the general gist.

Sounds dreamy, right? Though, really, experts say that the more disgusting and greener it looks, the better it tastes. So don't be expecting to be served a culinary work of art should you find yourself in Bradford and a steaming bowl of doodle soup in front of you. No records exist of how, when, or where the dish originated. Still, Bradford residents are more than happy to adopt it as their own.

Like elsewhere in Tennessee, if you have a noteworthy attribute, you promote the heck out of it and also hold an annual festival to secure this accomplishment; Bradford is no exception. Every third weekend of September welcomes the Doodle Soup Festival, put on by the Lions Club and benefiting underprivileged children in the area. You can expect to find every possible doodle recipe passed down through generations, available for sample. Festivities are not limited to all things doodle, however: You'll also find dog shows, a parade, costume displays, ice-cream-eating contests, and BBQ cook-offs.

Bradford is located 38 miles north of Jackson, off US 45 East. For more information on the festival, call Betty Jo Taylor, the event's founder, at (731) 742-3494.

A Strange Place for an Art Exhibit

Brownsville

Many people (myself included) will often pose the question: What is art? Is it a Jackson Pollock or a pile of trash on the side of the interstate? A rare Picasso or a three-year-old child's finger painting? Local boy (and artist) Billy Tripp will tell you it's his creation, the Mindfield, comprising an average of 80 vertical feet of twisting, turning steel. Located about an hour north of Memphis, the Mindfield spans an acre and grazes 125 feet at its tallest point. Tripp created it as his "life's work": It began in 1989 and will continue to be built upon until his death, at which point he's demanded to be buried at the site of his masterpiece.

If you look closely, you'll see a time line of Tripp's life: Various components represent monumental occurrences, such as the death of his father, Reverend Charles Tripp, in 2002, which is memorialized via a water tower that was transported from Kentucky down over the border and into Brownsville. All steel is recycled from nearby businesses and factories that have since closed. If you're passing through Brownsville in the summer months, there's a good chance you'll see Tripp tending to his muse, as his work often seems to be seasonal (makes sense—no one wants to be climbing scaffolding in the dead of a Tennessee winter).

To reach the Mindfield, head west on TN 54/19 from the Brownsville town square. The monument will be on the southeast corner of the intersection of TN 54/19 and US 70 South, at 1 Mindfield Alley. Entrance is free.

Pretty, Shiny Things
Camden

Tahiti and pearls are often considered synonymous, but Tennessee and pearls? Not so much (or not unless you're a pearl insider, that is). That said, you'll probably be surprised to find that the pearl is the state gem and for good reason: They're harvested from the freshwater mussels found in the state's fast-running rivers.

The whole concept started in the second half of the twentieth century when a man from Camden, John Latendresse, saw freshwater pearls being cultivated overseas. This was no coincidence, really, as John was married to a Japanese-born woman, and the Japanese were the first to cultivate pearls. The business-minded man returned home and spent ages seeking out the right water source with the perfect pH balance and, after researching practically every body of water across the United States, found it right near his own house: Kentucky Lake. He then created the pearl farm in 1980, though it was five years before the first mussels could be cracked open.

Unlike in other areas of the world where pearl farms are common, Tennessee pearls come in all different colors (not to mention shapes and sizes, too). While a handful may be used for fashion locally, the majority of harvested pearls are shipped overseas to Asia.

★ ★

The farm is located at the Birdsong Resort; there's even an accompanying free museum where you can learn about the history of the pearl farm operation and the cultivating process in depth. The Tennessee River Freshwater Pearl Museum, Farm, Tour, and Pearl Jewelry Showroom are all located at 255 Marina Rd. in Camden, 9 miles north of the Birdsong exit (exit 133) off I-40. For more information, call (731) 584-7880 or visit www.tennesseeriverpearls.com.

Blast from the Past
Collierville

When in Memphis, you'll hear a lot about Germantown, the city's biggest and most prominent burb, but you likely won't hear much about its neighbor, Collierville, located about 30 miles southeast of downtown Memphis. For good reason: There's not much there—save the city's quaint and charming old-timey square.

In this day and age, it's rare to find an old-fashioned downtown replete with such nostalgia as a soda fountain and a stagecoach stop, which is precisely why Collierville's Historic Town Square is such a rare gem.

★ ★

That alone, however, is fully worth the trek out to suburbia. It has boutiques and antiques stores; divine little eateries like the Silver Caboose, replete with an ancient soda fountain (www.silvercaboose .com); a '60s-style hamburger joint; and even an old-school gas station, McGinnis Oil Company, where attendants still come out and fill your tank for you. There's also a previously operating train depot and former stagecoach stop, dating back to the 1800s. It's like a trip back in time without even needing a DeLorean.

The Historic Town Square is located on Main Street in downtown Collierville. For more information, visit www.mainstreetcollierville.org.

Seeing in Color
Finger

It was more than a decade ago—1999 to be precise—when Victor Stoll and his family held the first MartinFest. The previous year, a handful of martin landlords, who had become friendly via the online Purple Martin Forum, convened at the Stoll estate to put names with faces, and word of the event spread. It quickly became an annual occurrence, an invitation extended to whomever wished to attend. Today more than 500 martin enthusiasts from all over the country gather for the occasion each June.

But what exactly is a martin, you might ask? (Don't feel silly if you don't know: I had to research it myself.) It's the largest North American swallow and a popular inhabitant of backyard birdhouses. Martins sport a coat of dark black feathers with a purple iridescence. Not only are they pretty, but they also serve as an organic pesticide, keeping insect populations under control. They are known to sing one beautiful song (it's part of their mystique).

Victor, who had previously lived in Belize and established a colony there, lays claim to the largest colony of purple martins in the world, with more than 600 breeding pairs. (Interestingly, his family is also well known for producing 8,000 gallons of sorghum a year, a task taken over by Victor's wife, Esther, and their children and grandchildren, due to his ailing health.) If you're in the area, drive by the Stoll farm for a vision of purple and black, or the most interesting sight, a family of martins nesting on a hearty gourd, a favorite perch of theirs that is one of the things that keep them migrating back each spring.

The farm is located in the town of Finger, 25 miles south of Jackson off TN 5 South/US 45 South. For more martin information, pick up a copy of *Stoll's Purple Martin Book* (Ora Stoll Publishing, 2009).

The BBQ Wars

Germantown

While exploring the culinary roots of West Tennessee, you'll probably hear about Rendezvous until the cows come home. Officially, it's the "best" barbecue in Memphis. At least, that's what tourists think. Unofficially, that honor goes to the Germantown Commissary on the city's outskirts, occupying a small, old commissary grocery storefront (aka an unassuming shack).

This rustic joint in a quiet section of Germantown—quiet except when a train passing nearby rattles everything, which only serves to further enhance the atmosphere—does it all: ribs, chicken, baked beans, sweet potato fries, coleslaw, deviled eggs, potato salad . . . the works. But you can't leave without trying the pulled pork—that would just plain be a sin. Many a Memphian will argue that the Commissary does the best straight-up barbecue sandwich in town, which is one tall order. And if the Web site's bold claims—"So good y'ull slap yo' mama," "Epicurean BBQ ribs, mmmm"—doesn't convince you, we're not sure what else will. Just be sure to save room for dessert, as lemon icebox pie, chocolate pie, caramel cake, coconut cake, coconut cream pie, and chocolate chip cheesecake all grace the menu.

In 2009 *Playboy* magazine went as far as to name the place one of the top ten barbecue joints in the country, claiming "the Commissary ups the quality quotient by making everything by hand, and its Monday all-you-can-eat ribs feeds into our penchant for gluttony." The place is always hoppin', so plan to visit during off-peak dining

★ ★

hours or be subjected to a possible thirty-minute wait (maybe more on weekends).

Other popular BBQ restaurants are Corky's, a local-chain-gone-national that has its own supermarket line of hearty sauces; Rendez-vous, which most locals will tell you is overrated; and Central, which gets our second-place vote for best barbecue around. The Commissary is located at 2290 Germantown Road in Germantown. For more information, visit www.commissarybbq.com.

No Voodoo for You

Everywhere you go in downtown Memphis, you'll see signs pointing you toward palm readers and fortune-tellers. Voodoo dolls and beads fill many of the curiosity shops. It's no New Orleans, but fortune-telling is still one of the city's biggest shticks. But on the outskirts, in its biggest suburb of Germantown—don't even go there. All forms of the aforementioned—or "to predict or foretell future events or the fate of future acts or fortunes of any nation, business, group or person or individual"—are strictly forbidden by local statute. This includes "analysis of parts, products or personal characteristics of a person, or by analysis of any animate or inanimate object including, but not limited to, celestial body, crystal ball, tea leaves, or playing or other cards, or through the exercise of any purported psychic, mediumistic, prophetic, occult, clairvoyant or supernatural power." So before you set up your table and a deck of tarot cards on a corner in downtown Germantown, remember: You have been warned.

A Tree Grows in Greenfield

Greenfield

Home to Big Cypress Tree State Park and the annual Big Cypress Fall Festival—which comprises birds of prey programs, live music, and arts and crafts—Greenfield used to have yet another grand honor to its name: It was once the home of the largest bald cypress tree in the whole country, and the biggest tree of any kind east of the Mississippi. The tree grew to a sturdy 40 feet around and lived to be a wise 1,350 years before a lightning bolt struck it in 1976, causing it to reach an untimely demise. But even after its death, it continued to display its widely known omnipotence by smoking and burning for a solid two weeks after the strike.

While ye olde tree no longer rules over Greenfield, there are still plenty of reasons to spend the afternoon lounging in the 330-acre park. Numerous hiking trails are one, picnicking in the shelter and making use of recreational play structures for the kidlets are a couple others. The forestry major will also get a kick out of putting his education to use and trying to decipher between the sycamores, sweet gums, bald cypresses, river birches, and various kinds of oaks along the tree identification path. Wildflowers, shrubs, hummingbirds, and butterflies complete the picturesque scene.

From Jackson, take US 45 East north through Greenfield, turn left on TN 445 (Kimery Store Road), and follow the road for approximately 5 miles to the natural area entrance on the right. For more information, call (731) 235-2700.

Caution: Rodent Crossing

Kenton

Another town with an oddball boasting is 1,400-person Kenton, straddling the line of Obion and Gibson Counties. It's extremely proud of its furry inhabitants, the albino (or white) squirrel—so much so that its border is marked with a HOME OF THE WHITE SQUIRREL tagline and picture.

★ ★

There really is no difference between an albino squirrel and a regular ol' squirrel, other than the color of its coat. About 200 of the rare breed, which allegedly were left behind by a Gypsy caravan shortly after the Civil War, roam the verdant paths and lawns of Kenton. Even if you don't see the white squirrel itself (which you should if you've got your bifocals handy), you'll find a plethora of related paraphernalia around town: The town mascot decorates everything from street crossing warnings to KENTON IS TOO BEAUTIFUL TO LITTER signs.

Three other towns in the United States—Brevard, North Carolina; Marionville, Missouri; and Onley, Illinois—also claim to be the world albino squirrel headquarters. Who reigns supreme? I'll leave that up for you to decide.

Kenton is located about 48 miles north of Jackson off US 45 West.

Beans, Beans, They're Good for Your Heart
Martin

Every small town from here to Timbuktu has its own weird festival; it's almost like a rite of passage. Martin proves no exception to the rule.

Paying their respects to the "Magic Bean," Martin natives get tickled pink around mid-September every year when all other action in town comes to a screeching halt in observance of the nine-day Soybean Festival. There are pancake breakfasts, carnival rides, merchant sidewalk sales, library brown-bag lunches and readings, art exhibits, the Miss Soybean Beauty Pageant, golf tourneys, free concerts by artists like Sister Hazel or Lonestar, street fairs, and lots of bingo. And let's not forget about the Soybean Idol contest, in which forty crooners take the stage at UT Martin to compete for the gold. Where does the soybean factor in all of that? I have absolutely no idea.

For more information on the Soybean Festival, call (731) 588-2507 or visit www.tnsoybeanfestival.org.

★ ★

The King Lives
Memphis

I'd be remiss to pen an entire section on Memphis and not talk about its most famous past inhabitant: Elvis Presley. His presence is everywhere: in the statue on South Main Street, in the halls of Sun Studio, on the walls at the Peanut Shoppe, in nearly every diner booth or eating establishment that was around during his lifetime (the owners, they all have their Elvis stories). And everyone from Alaska to Timbuktu knows about his famous home, Graceland.

However, if you really want to see a tried-and-true tribute to him, skip Graceland entirely and head 50 miles southeast of Memphis to Holly Springs, Mississippi, where one of the biggest shrines to Elvis—called "Graceland Too"—remains. The museum's creator and caretaker, Paul McLeod, runs the place, never sleeping, always chugging back a can of Coke (he says he goes through a twenty-four pack a day), and keeping his home open all day, every day, should someone be driving through and want to stop and take a gander. All you have to do is knock on his front door and fork over a minuscule donation to be transported to Elvis Land. The house's exterior is a Pepto Bismol shade of pink and contains every bit of Elvis-related memorabilia one could come up with, a fifty-year obsession that cost Paul his job, multiple homes, several cars, and a wife. (His wife gave him an ultimatum—it was her or Elvis. Paul chose the latter.)

Fanatic is not a strong enough word to describe Paul's love for Elvis. He even named his only son Elvis Aaron Presley McLeod. The inside of the house is wallpapered with Elvis clippings and LPs (both the covers and the discs themselves); doorways are adorned with Elvis-patterned curtains. More than 31,000 tapes of video footage stream nonstop on eight different TVs. The ceiling of the TV room is covered with baseball card–like Elvis photos. Other sorts of things you'll find inside the museum include a carpet sample from Graceland's famed Jungle Room, Elvis's high school yearbook in which they

11

★ ★

misspelled his name, and a handful of guitars allegedly used by the King.

Graceland Too is located at 200 East Gholson Ave. in Holly Springs.

Although he's been dead for more than thirty years, the rock 'n' roll crooner known as Elvis still has a presence in every last neighborhood within Memphis, particularly downtown.

Take a Holiday
Memphis

While local boy Kemmons Wilson was on a long, exhausting family road trip to the nation's capital in 1951, a lightbulb went on in his head. As if the stifling summer heat and traveling with five squawking kids weren't enough, Wilson was appalled at the lack of quality service and, more importantly, consistency as he and his family bopped from one roadside motel to the next. He knew something needed to be done, and sooner rather than later, to remedy this, so he made it his life's mission to do just that. In 1952, just a year after that fateful road trip, the first of Kemmons's chain of now popular hotels—the Holiday Inn franchise—opened in Memphis.

Kemmons's brilliant idea morphed into more than 1,600 properties worldwide, though in the 1970s the brand began to decline (it's probably no coincidence either that its founder retired at the close of that decade). And, as Kemmons would have told you up until his death in 2003, the changing of the sign and logo in 1982 following his retirement was the worst mistake the company could have ever made. Still, it's probably one of the most recognized hotel chains around the globe, and it all started in Memphis.

Alas, you can no longer visit the original establishment; it was torn down at the turn of the millennia and transformed into a funeral home. RIP first Holiday Inn. RIP Kemmons Wilson.

The Peanut Man
Memphis

Five minutes in the downtown staple Peanut Shoppe will reveal one thing: There's not a soul in Memphis who owner Rida Abuzaineh does not know. Every last Tom, Dick, and Harry who enters the door is greeted by name; Rida even knows what many of them want to order before they quite know themselves. The Jerusalem-born entrepreneur came to Memphis two decades ago by way of Long Beach, California, to purchase one of Memphis's most legendary establishments from the Planters Nuts legacy.

Back in the 1940s, there were more than 200 such shops sprinkled around the country, but they began to wane in popularity and started to shutter and sale in the '50s and '60s. Today there are only seven of these once widely favored shops remaining, two of which are located in Memphis: Rida's Main Street storefront (by far the more popular of the two) and another located on Sumner Avenue.

Trinkets and memorabilia from the golden days of Planters remain on the shop's shelves and walls as reminders of the company's past, including original peanut-adorned wallpaper from the 1950s. It's even said that back in the shop's glory days, Elvis was a fan: The owner at the time was said to have kicked him out frequently for flirting with all the ladies inside.

Rida can be credited for the Peanut Shoppe's regaining its long-lost popularity; he mans the hot spot with his wife, Ameerah, and no doubt the store's loyal following is due to the charm and kindness of the charismatic duo. At eighteen years, they've owned it longer than any other owners, the Planters family included, and have been featured on many TV stations, including the Food Network.

Aside from fresh-roasted peanuts daily—you can even see the eighty-one-year-old roaster (in the form of the Planters Nuts mascot, naturally) in the front of the store—Rida and Ameerah sell a variety of fare, from chocolate-coated raisins, pistachios, chocolate stars, and malt balls to rock candy, Brach's root beer barrels, and Rida's personal favorite, a rainbow of candy fruit slices. I challenge you to leave the establishment without a mixed bag of all the delights. They're also not stingy with their goods and will let you sample before you buy. Prices are very reasonable given the demand. Just don't expect to stop in for a quick visit: Rida's colorful stories will have you wanting to stick around all day just listening.

The Peanut Shoppe is located at 24 South Main St. in downtown Memphis. For more information, call (901) 525-1115 or log onto www.memphispeanutshoppe.com.

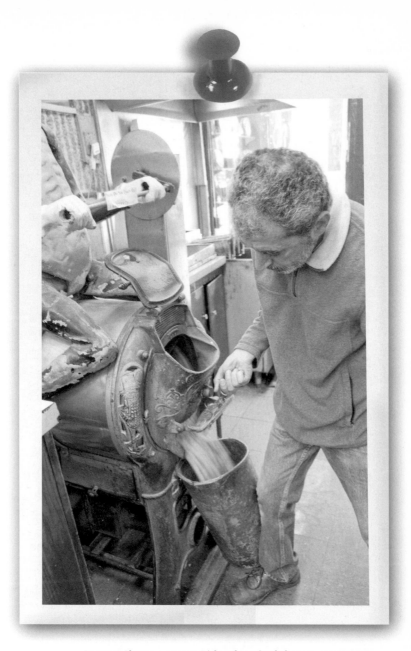

Peanut Shoppe owner Rida Abuzaineh keeps customers
happy by maintaining a piping hot supply of peanuts,
fresh from the old 1920s roaster.

Going to the Ducks

Memphis

The legendary Peabody Hotel has likely hosted every famous figure to travel through Memphis in its 142 years of existence. While a few other boutique hotels have opened in the recent past, it will always be the city's grande dame. Still, there are few hotel guests—or city residents for that matter—who are more cherished and popular than the Peabody's daily entertainers: the ducks. Led by a human ring-leader, of course, they make their daily waddle from the penthouse down the elevator, along the red carpet (which is littered with tour-ists and non–hotel guests on every occasion), to the central fountain in the lobby, where they're more than happy to splash around and cheekily pose for photos.

But where did they come from? And why are they there? The story goes that the general manager in 1933, Frank Schutt, returned to town after a hunting trip and, having spent a little too much time with his good pal Jack Daniels, decided to cook up a little mischief. His idea of a practical joke was to let some of the live duck decoys loose in the foun-tain. But what he meant as a prank was an instant smash hit with the guests, and the hotel decided to keep the ducks around as its mascots. (According to the Peabody Web site, however, the ducks weren't the fountain's first inhabitants: For a brief period in the 1920s, turtles and baby alligators allegedly patrolled the waters.)

Five North American mallards soon replaced the original three English call ducks, and to this day the ducks circle the marble fountain at 11:00 a.m. and 5:00 p.m. daily. When the Marching Ducks aren't working—aside from their regular duties (i.e., entertaining the guests), they also make TV appearances, having been featured on such shows as *Sesame Street, The Oprah Winfrey Show,* and *The Tonight Show with Johnny Carson*—they relax in their Royal Duck Palace on the rooftop.

The theme spans to the lavish hotel rooms: Soap bars are shaped like ducks, and all the toiletries and linens bear the recognizable insig-nia as well. Rooms are old-fashioned, with dressed-up amenities like

The iconic Peabody Hotel is famous for more than just its
sumptuous digs: It's also home to some of the city's most
famed residents, the Marching Ducks, who make their
twice-daily march down to the lobby from the roof.

COURTESY OF THE PEABODY HOTEL

flat-screen TVs, and worthy of a night's stay. The resident restaurant,
Chez Philippe, is divine, as well as possibly the only French restaurant
in the world where you won't find—you guessed it—duck anywhere
on the menu.

The Peabody is located at 149 Union Ave. in downtown Memphis.
For more information, call (901) 529-4000 or visit www.peabody
memphis.com.

★ ★

Islands in the Stream
Memphis

The last place you might expect to find a thriving island is in downtown Memphis, a city in the middle of a landlocked region of the United States. But stranger things have happened in these parts than an islet in the middle of the muddy Mississippi River becoming a major tourist attraction.

There's so much to do on this prosperous little stretch of land, appropriately named Mud Island, that you could easily lose yourself there for an entire day. You can rent kayaks or canoes, bicycles or paddleboats. You can stroll along the River Walk, with its five-block replica of the lower part of the river, or drop by the Mississippi River Museum. If you're visiting on the second Friday of the month between April and October, feel free to claim your plot of land and

Situated in the Mississippi River below the De Soto Bridge, bustling Mud Island has enough fun-filled family activities to fill an entire day and then some.

★ ★

pitch a tent (provided by the recreation committee) for Sleep Out on the Mississippi, a popular camping extravaganza.

Mud Island River Park is located just west of downtown Memphis in the Mississippi River, directly below I-40 and the Hernando de Soto Bridge. Access to the island itself is free, though there are nominal fees for most of the attractions and rentals. To get there, you can go by foot via the walkway (located above the monorail) or take the Mud Island Monorail from 125 North Front St. in downtown Memphis. For more information, call (800) 507-6507 or visit www.mudisland.com.

This Little Piggy Went to the Market
Memphis

Virginia-born Clarence Saunders dropped out of school early on to work as a clerk in a general store toward the end of the nineteenth century. This was a harbinger of what his future would hold, as he went from salesman for a wholesale grocer as a young teen, to working for a grocery co-op in his later youth, to starting one of the biggest grocery store franchises in history.

Twenty years after Clarence first clerked, he started a grocery wholesaler that sold for cash only. A year later, in 1916, he opened the Piggly Wiggly, the first self-service grocery in the country, which allowed customers to select the items they wanted from the aisles and take them up to the front counter to pay. Clarence patented the concept the following year. In less than five years, he managed to expand his brand from one to more than 1,000 stores in nearly thirty states. How's that for the entrepreneurial spirit?

With his sizable income, Clarence began building a garish pink mansion in Memphis (see the "This and That" entry) that he later had to sell when the stock market forced him into bankruptcy. The Piggly Wiggly chain still thrives to this day in parts of the United States, primarily smaller towns in the Southeast. While nowhere near as big as it once was, "the Pig," as it's often called, operates more than 600 stores in seventeen states. The original Piggly Wiggly was located at 79 Jefferson St. in downtown Memphis.

★ ★

There's No Cake Like a Cupcake

Memphis

Sure, the cupcake trend has taken hold of big cities like New York
and San Francisco, leaving many a resident just a little bit fatter but
no doubt happier, but it took longer for the craze to seep into other
corners of the country, which was perhaps a good thing, as it allowed
companies like Muddy's Bake Shop to not only perfect the art of the
cupcake, but far outdo its competitors with style and creativity while
at it.

Following in the footsteps of the country's burgeoning cupcake trend, Muddy's Bake Shop prides itself on serving some
of the most delicious and creative baked goods around.

Cupcakes at Muddy's aren't just straight-up chocolate or vanilla (though, for the traditionalist, they've got those, too), but rather a list of twenty or so different varieties each week, such as the Capote, chocolate cake with vanilla buttercream frosting and sprinkles; Oode-lolly, vanilla cake with coconut filling and old-fashioned boiled icing and shaved coconut on top; Monkey Around, banana cake with pecans and banana icing; the Grasshopper, chocolate cake with green peppermint icing; the King, banana cake with peanut butter icing; or the signature Prozac, which is always on the menu and is simply chocolate cake with creamy chocolate buttercream icing.

They've also got delicious pies and cookies and regular ol' cakes and even a daily vegan special—plus a short menu of lunch items, too—should you be a weirdo who doesn't like cupcakes. The inside of the fairly large shop is decorated in a whimsical Alice in Wonderland sort of theme, fulfilling every little girl's dream to have a spot of tea and treat in such a fairytale-like place.

Muddy's Bake Shop is located at 5101 Sanderlin at number 114 in the shopping center. For more information, call (901) 683-8844 or visit www.muddysbakeshop.com.

This and That
Memphis

A hodgepodge of local trivia and memorabilia, the Pink Palace com-prises a number of unconnected Memphis exhibits. Built by Piggly Wiggly founder Clarence Saunders, it's no wonder you can mosey through a replica of the country's first-ever self-service store, or you can read more about the yellow fever epidemic that swept the city in the nineteenth century. You can't miss the building either: It's a large marble edifice that is totally painted in—you guessed it—pink (save a green roof).

In addition to a four-story-high IMAX facility, there's a 165-seater theater inside the Sharpe Planetarium that features a number of shows on the dome ceiling, from meteor showers to laser light

★ ★

productions. You'll also find a nature center with live mammals, reptiles, and birds, and a science center that traces history through fossils.

Every Christmas the Pink Palace features the Enchanted Forest Festival of Trees, a collection of twenty or so trees each with unique themes designed by local organizations. Recently there was a University of Memphis–themed tree designed by the alumni association, a "Beat of Memphis" music-themed tree designed by a cardiology team, and a "What a Girl Wants" tree designed by high school cheerleaders. Booths and displays on the holiday celebrations of countries all over the world are also featured.

The Pink Palace Family of Museums is located at 3050 Central Ave. in midtown Memphis. For more information, call (901) 320-6320 or visit www.memphismuseums.org.

Oral History
Memphis

The Center for Southern Folklore is carefully wedged among all the kitsch and touristy attractions that dot Main Street—so carefully wedged, in fact, that you might not even notice it upon first glance. But take a second look. A nonprofit organization, the center is supported by the Tennessee Arts Commission and is chock-full of goodies.

The aim of the center is to showcase the South's glorious culture—its food, traditions, arts, stories, and music—through a series of art exhibits, documentaries, live music, and the like. Funky decor fills the entire establishment, as do black-and-white photographs of Delta musicians, farmers, artisans, and other Southerners with a craft to boast. Best of all, you can visit for free (though there's a cover for some of the nighttime bands).

Additionally, there's a an easygoing cafe housed in the amazingly colorful shop should you need to break from all the culture for a cup o' joe, and a 250-seat dining room upstairs where the main performance venue in Peabody Place is located. Sampling the yummy fare such as the well-known peach cobbler is a must. If live music isn't your thing and all you're looking for is a token of your time in Memphis, the center will also fit that bill nicely. It's got an eclectic smattering of offerings in the ground-level shop. If you happen to be passing through over Labor Day weekend, you'll be double blessed: The center sponsors the annual Memphis Music and Heritage Fest, which always promises a rousing good time.

You'll find a chalkboard of upcoming events at the front of the folklore store. The main office and folklore hall are located at 119 South Main St. For more information, visit www.southernfolklore.com.

The splashy Center for Southern Folklore is a great place to experience the food, tradition, arts, and stories of the glorious South.

★ ★

Friend or Foe?

Today Memphis is Tennessee's largest city, with well over one million residents in its metropolitan area, but that wasn't always the case. It took years for it to become the civilized, sprawling cultural mecca it is at present. It was such a slow process, in fact, that the city's founders didn't even manage to reap the benefits of their investment. What's worse is that for a few decades running, it had a rival just 40 miles upstream serving as a constant thorn in its side.

In the early 1800s a town called Randolph, located where the Big Hatchee River pours into the Mississippi River, was in stark competition with Memphis for the title of Tennessee's biggest city. With just 1,000 residents, it claimed more than fifty businesses, a tavern, six dry goods stores, ten physicians, four hotels, and over ten saloons. It was touch-and-go there for a while as Randolph continued to thrive and showed no signs of slowing down, but lucky for Memphis, the railroad came to town, making it a much more convenient spot for West Tennessee farmers to come sell their cotton for it to be sent out on boats. Simultaneously, during the Civil War, Union troops destroyed Randolph, and much of the town was never rebuilt, leaving it an unincorporated rural community of just 200 people today.

Pedal to the Metal

Memphis

Ask a Memphian how to reach the Ornamental Metal Museum, and there's a good chance he'll respond with a blank stare and "Huh? The ornamental what?" That's because these riverside grounds that flank the Mississippi are so well hidden, many locals don't even realize

The only museum of its kind in the country, the Ornamental Metal Museum showcases a number of different installations and metalworking methods— from art pieces to jewelry to furniture.

they're there. But don't let that deter you: It's the only metal museum in the entire country and well worth a visit.

Occupying a former military hospital, the museum spills over into three side-by-side buildings. The one closest to the entrance is where you'll buy your ticket, take in the latest rotating exhibit, and likely spend a few dollars on artistic ware. (I walked out with a hammered pewter

Ribbet, Ribbet

Tennessee has some oddball laws, but one of the weirdest is more off the wall than the rest: In Memphis, it's illegal for frogs to croak after 11:00 p.m. Yes, you read that right. Those little green buggers are legally required to keep their ribbets under wraps. So the next time you're burning the midnight oil and run into a croaker, do your citizenly duty and tell him to keep his trap shut.

As if that weren't enough, here are some other local laws that have me scratching my head in awe (or is it confusion?): It's illegal for a woman to drive a car unless a man is either running or walking in front of the vehicle waving a red flag to warn approaching motorists and pedestrians (no, I'm sadly not joking . . . Memphis has yet to be over-taken by women's lib, clearly), as well as illegal to take unfinished pie home from a restaurant.

Lucky for you and me (and the frogs), none of these odd laws are enforced any longer, yet one still remains: All panhandlers have to have a permit before asking for money, according to the Memphis City Council. The fine for panhandling is around $50, but the permit is free. How's that for irony?

ring and a bronze wire piece titled *Sisters* for my house; I could have left with a whole lot more.) Littering the grounds are various installations, each one as different and more fascinating than the next. The big white house in the back is home to the permanent pieces and library, and to its left is the blacksmith shop, where you can see the resident smiths blazing custom-made bed frames, chandeliers, benches, and the like. Be sure to check out the gazebo in the backyard, as it offers some of the best unobstructed views of the Mississippi River around.

The museum is so off the beaten path that it takes a little searching. Located at 374 Metal Museum Dr., it's easiest to take I-55 North toward St. Louis and get off at the last exit before the bridge, exit 12C, then follow the exit road to the museum. Just be sure to get in the interstate's right lane in advance, lest you find yourself in Arkansas. It's the last exit before leaving the state, and the first one when arriving. For more information, call (901) 774-6380 or visit www.metalmuseum .org.

Seeing Stars
Memphis

Formerly a shoddy, rundown hood where no sane person would venture unescorted after the railroad industry's decline in the 1970s, the onetime ghost town known as the South Main Arts District houses some of Memphis's best-known attractions—such as the National Civil Rights Museum and the Arcade diner—at its most bustling intersection, South Main Street and G. E. Patterson. It's also a mecca for dive bars and juke joints.

On top of all that, it's home to dozens of movie sets, from *Black Snake Moan, 21 Grams,* and *Hustle and Flow* to Southern author John Grisham's novels-turned-big-screen-delights *The Client* and *The Firm.* Sporadic placards in the area designate what movies and scenes were filmed where, and every restaurant and bar owner has some (perhaps embellished) tale of all the celebrities he considers among his inner circle of friends. *(See photo next page)*

Once a rundown neighborhood where no sane person would venture for fun, South Main is no longer up and coming—it's already there. You'll find some of your best restaurants and dive bars stocking its corridors.

The Five and Diner

Memphis

At the Arcade, one of Memphis's longest-running breakfast establishments—it's touted as the oldest, having been opened in 1919 by a Grecian immigrant, then reopened in 1925 as a Greek-revival joint, then finally turned into a diner in the '50s—the hotly contested debate is just what exactly the signature dish is. The Food Network swears it's the sweet potato pancakes (with which I'm inclined to agree), while the Travel Channel puts its money on the Eggs Redneck, smothered in country gravy (didn't try it, so can't offer my two cents). Either way, you really can't go wrong. Both dishes, like all the combination platters, are served with biscuits, hash browns or grits, and bacon or sausage—you have no chance of leaving the old-school diner the slightest bit hungry.

The Arcade serves lunch and dinner, too, but you'd be crazy to order any meal other than breakfast. It's got what we Southerners consider the ultimate trifecta: good food, good Southern hospitality, and good ol' Southern comfort. And if the diner's facade looks familiar, it's for good reason: The Arcade has made cameos in such flicks as *Walk the Line* and *Mystery Train*. Speaking of stars, you'll also be able to sit in some of their favorite booths, such as the ones frequented by JFK and the King himself.

The Arcade is located on 540 South Main St. at G. E. Patterson in Memphis's South Main district. For more information, call (901) 526-5757 or log onto www.arcaderestaurant.com.

Battle of the Breakfasts: With the Best Breakfast Dish in Memphis still up for grabs, the Arcade has two strong contenders, the Eggs Redneck and the sweet potato pancakes. You decide which is deserving of such an accolade.

Your Meter's Running

No one likes to feed the parking meter—I get that. But the South Main Arts District makes parking just a tad bit more fun with a whole slew of creatively splattered meters.

Along South Main Street from Linden Avenue to G. E. Patterson, you'll spot a dozen or so meters that were transformed from their dull gray hue to bold patterns and colors by local artists. One even makes use of a vintage bowling league trophy. Take a few minutes to visit them all before choosing your favorite and carrying on with your day as planned.

In keeping with South Main's artistic flair, even the parking meters have a creative quality about them—each one different (and more garish) than the last.

A Bar with a Story

Memphis

It may not look like much from the outside, but don't let that deter you from taking a peek into Earnestine and Hazel's lair. Few Memphis bars have more history than this trendy dive. Way back when, it was indeed a brothel. There's no hiding this fact, and owner Russell George will proudly tell you the whole time line of the joint. Before that even, it was a thriving drugstore. But in the 1950s a pair of spunky sisters— named, you guessed it, Earnestine and Hazel—purchased the place.

When Earnestine and Hazel started welcoming talented yet unknown musicians to play at their place at night, it became a

This South Main dive has been a haunt of many a famous musician, as well as the scene for several Hollywood blockbusters.

★ ★

bustling dance hall of sorts, and eventually the bar helped spark the careers of many musical greats. Big names said to frequent the joint include Ike and Tina Turner, Otis Redding, Solomon Burke, and, yes, even the King himself. Then, years after the blues era came and went and the rail industry retreated, the South Main district became a mere afterthought—that is, until Russell George got his hands on the place in the early '90s and turned it back around.

The bar has had its time in the spotlight, too, appearing in many movies, such as *Elizabethtown* and *Rainmaker*. Through his job as owner/manager, Russell has added a few celebrities to his inner circle of friends, including Jon Voight, with whom he spent a lot of time while the actor was shooting a film in town. The cast even eschewed its original plan of a fancy Peabody wrap party to rock out at Earnestine & Hazel's with Russell. Memorabilia, photographs, and press clippings line the wall in a visual time line of the bar's existence.

It's definitely a spot you want to check off your list, whether you go during daylight hours or after the clock's struck midnight. And thanks to the world-famous Soul Burgers, which are constantly on the fryer, your belly will stay full while you continue to quench your thirst. (The grill stays open as late as the dance floor, into the wee hours of the morning, so it's also prime real estate for late-night eats.)

Earnestine & Hazel's is located at 531 South Main St. in downtown Memphis. For more information, call (901) 523-9754 or visit www .earnestineandhazels.com.

Musical Mojo
Memphis

Tired of the same old boring tour? Want a guided view of Memphis, sans the droning of some old fogy who is disenchanted with his job and his life and has been doing the same thing day in, day out, since around the time you were born? That's where Backbeat Tours comes in. Helmed by a group of local musicians, the hip tour guide company provides musical safaris through one of the country's most melodic cities by singing you through the motions.

It's a campy sing-along, but taken at face value (and trust me, none of the Backbeat guys take themselves seriously), it can be a whole heck of a lot of fun. All guides play the guitar as well, and guests, who are given a tambourine or shaker upon boarding the bus, are encouraged to join in the fun. The mode of transportation is another fun facet of the trip: You're toted around town in a kitted-out '50s-style school bus dubbed "Miss Clawdy" with a shiny red veneer and Naugahyde seat covers.

The Mojo Tour is likely the most popular of the company's offerings, as it visits famed landmarks like the Wonderbread bakery, Cotton Row, movie locations, and Lauderdale Court, where Elvis grew up. Aside from Mojo, the standard Historic Memphis Walking Tour, and a Ghost Tour, there's also the Hound Dog Tour and Graceland Tour.

Backbeat Tours is located at 140 Beale St. in downtown Memphis. For more information, call (866) 392-2328 or visit www.backbeat tours.com.

A Ghost Town
Memphis

Just the facade of the Orpheum Theater, especially on a gloomy day, looks like it could easily be home to the supernatural. And it is—or so the story goes. The interior is decked out with elegant finishes like chandeliers, and you almost get the sense that this is the sort of place Andrew Lloyd Webber was writing about when he penned *Phantom of the Opera*. Only this time, the perpetrator's not a masked man in black, but a sad little girl who goes by the name of Mary.

Mary's sobs and shuffling have long been heard by theater techs; her white nightgown sweeping across the floor has frequently been seen by many. As she was "spotted" or heard more regularly, people at the theater started to freak out over her presence—though she was a gentle spirit who seemed to harbor no ill will or have malicious intent—so a group of parapsychology students entered the scene.

★ ★

After performing a series of séances, the students deduced that Mary was a former vaudevillian who died in a traumatic accident downtown in the 1920s. Her love for the theater attracted her to live her postmortem days in the Orpheum, and she weeps out of loneliness. So if you're wandering the back corridors of the Orpheum alone at night and hear a gentle sobbing, fear not: It's just your friendly theater ghost.

The Orpheum Theater is located at 203 South Main St. It still puts on concerts and musicals today; Mary is just an added attraction. For more information, call (901) 525-3000 or visit www.orpheum-memphis.com.

The iconic Orpheum Theater continues to host a number of concerts and musical productions—just be wary of Mary, its longtime ghostly inhabitant.

The Cursed Bedroom

Memphis's spooky past doesn't end at the Orpheum Theater. Up the road in the Victorian Village Historic District is where the Woodruffs once resided, in what was accurately called Millionaire's Row at the time. The father, Amos, a carriage maker, built his family an opulent mansion in the neighborhood in 1871. The eldest child, Mollie, continued to live in the house even long after she married.

The Woodruffs' lifetime coincided with Memphis's deadly yellow fever epidemic that claimed the lives of thousands; one of Mollie's children, her first, fell ill with the disease at just three days old and died shortly thereafter in the second-floor bedroom. But Mollie's unlucky streak didn't stop there: After her husband caught pneumonia in a boating accident, he also passed away in that very room. Years later, well into her second marriage, Mollie had another child who died of yellow fever in the cursed bedroom.

Twelve years after Amos built the house, he sold it. But that didn't keep Mollie from returning to 680 Adams Ave. after she died in 1917. Many visitors to the old home claim they have seen a sad-looking woman all decked out in nineteenth-century garb rocking back and forth in a chair, and they are further shocked when they tell this to the curator only to find no other women were present in the house at the time—and the curator goes on to say she often has to tidy up rumpled bed linens, even when she made the bed just an hour before and no one else was home. Several psychics have run diagnostics on the room and upon finishing were not only able to pick the mysterious woman out in a lineup, but were also able to describe in vivid detail the clothing she wore—with no chance of ever having seen such a garment firsthand.

The Woodruff-Fontaine House is open to visitors. It hosts group tours, teas, parties, and even a ghost tour from time to time. For more information, call (901) 526-1469 or visit www.woodruff-fontaine.com.

The Cabbage Patch

Memphis

Cabbage, that's what Alcenia's is known for. That and the giant squishy hugs and occasional smooch generously doled out by owner Betty Joyce "BJ" Chester-Tamayo (how's that for a mouthful?) every time a customer enters the door, or leaves for that matter. You really can't visit Alcenia's without feeling the overwhelming love and gratitude BJ has for every last one of her patrons. But, oddly enough, Alcenia's restaurant was first born out of tragedy. BJ lost her only son in a terrible accident and needed to do something with her time to fill the void and get her mind off of her broken heart. So she turned to what she knows best—soul food—and decided to make a career out of it by opening a restaurant.

The interior itself is an interesting amalgamation of bridal veil lace, beaded curtains, and primitive folk art, but the focus is all Southern, all the time. BJ takes traditional regional cuisine and adds a heavy hand of spices and herbs to such dishes as sweet potato fries, baked catfish, fried green tomatoes, and BBQ chicken. She's also started bottling some of her creations, such as her apple butter and signature "cha cha" (a relish made from cabbage, peppers, and tomatoes).

Speaking of, back to the cabbage. Yes, indeedy, that's the main attraction. For such a normally ho-hum dish, BJ injects a certain "wow" factor into the leafy vegetable by flavoring it with a mix of jerk chicken seasoning and lots of pepper, giving it a tongue-searing kick. To temper the scorching flavor, you'll also be served a basket of moist, melt-in-your-mouth cornbread. If your arteries aren't clogged yet, order one of everything on the dessert menu. Between sweet potato pie, BJ's famous bread pudding, and egg custard, you're not going to be able to choose just one.

Alcenia's is located at 317 North Main St. in downtown Memphis. For more information, call (901) 523-0200 or visit www.alcenias.com.

"I Have a Dream"

Memphis

It may not be the most upbeat of Memphis attractions, but the National Civil Rights Museum is, no doubt, one of the most beloved and educational sites there is. It's hard to wander through four centuries' worth of history and not feel moved. The museum backs the historic Lorraine Motel, where Martin Luther King Jr. was a frequent guest and where he was assassinated while in town to support striking sanitation workers; it continued to welcome visitors even after the bloody death until it was foreclosed in 1982.

The historic Lorraine Motel was where Martin Luther King Jr. spent his last minutes before being murdered in cold blood. It's now part of the National Civil Rights Museum.

Many monuments around Memphis pay homage to Martin Luther King Jr., but few are as packed with information as the National Civil Rights Museum.

Inside the museum you'll find a pictorial journey from the earliest slave revolts in 1619, to the boycotts in the 1950s and '60s, to MLK's death at the end of the museum trail. The room where MLK was murdered is set up as it was that fateful night in 1968 and is on display in the museum, and his final days are well-documented to the hour. Replicas of MLK's jail cell and the infamous Rosa Park bus are also on display. Significant court cases, protests, and sit-ins are covered at length, and the whole place is an overwhelming exhibit of emotion.

The National Civil Rights Museum is located at 450 Mulberry St. in downtown Memphis. For more information, call (901) 521-9699 or visit www.civilrightsmuseum.org.

Roller Girls
Memphis

Fitting in perfectly with the city's alternative-y vibe, Memphis Roller Derby has garnered quite a following, with an audience of 700 or more not an unusual turnout on bout days. The three local league teams—Women of Mass Destruction, PrisKilla Prezleys, and Angels of Death—play regularly against each other and teams from out of town, with the all-star team, the Memphis Hustlin' Rollers, which consists of la crème de la crème of derby girls, traveling the country to advance to regionals and sometimes beyond.

If you're not familiar with roller derby, a game that has been played in one form or another since 1922, the concept is quite simple: Each team sends five players onto the track in a pack. All start skating counterclockwise, keeping in a pack for the first lap. After crossing the line where they started, the jam begins. For two minutes both teams attempt to score as many points as possible with each team's jammer, who earns a lap for each person she passes after lapping the pack one time. The other two positions, the blockers and the pivot, do what they can to assist the jammer in her scoring follies.

While there are maneuvers that are considered illegal, refs tend to let the gals roughhouse (within reason); i.e., there aren't a whole lot of fouls called in derby. Games (or bouts, as they're called in derby-speak) consist of two thirty-minute periods. Got it? Good. (If you're still a bit fuzzy on the specifics and want the CliffsNotes version, take a couple hours to watch the Drew Barrymore movie *Whip It* before your first bout.)

Bouts occur throughout most of the year and are open to the public. League tryouts take place each winter and are open to skaters of all levels—in fact, you don't even have to be experienced on skates to come out and join in on the fun. For more information, visit www .memphisrollerderby.com.

Clang, Clang, Clang Goes the Trolley

Memphis

While Memphis is sorely lacking in the public transit arena, don't be surprised if you're meandering down Main Street on foot and hear the tinkling of bells alerting you to get out of the way. While it doesn't cover a very large area, the Memphis Area Transit Authority Trolley does have three lines that crisscross their way around downtown Memphis.

You won't get where you're going very fast—in fact, you could easily beat the trolley in a footrace, perhaps even lapping it a time

A handful of old-fashioned trolley cars from all over the world travel up and down South Main Street all day long. They're not speedy, but they're cheap and a Memphis must.

or two—which is why you won't see a whole lot of locals filling the seats. But visitors not on a schedule like to take them, particularly since it's similar to the San Francisco streetcar experience without the ridiculous lines, especially the Main Street route, which covers 2.5 miles of the most visited section of downtown. There's also the scenic Riverfront Loop and the Madison Avenue route, and a total of thirty-five stations and stops distributed among the three.

Fare is just a dollar, but it's free between 11:00 a.m. and 1:00 p.m. daily. Also free is the Art Trolley Tour on the last Friday of every month from 6:00 to 9:00 p.m., where locals and those passing through are encouraged to go out on the town, sip a glass of vino, sample some Southern cuisine, and browse the district's surplus of shops. The cars are as authentic as they look, too: The originals were imported from Portugal, and all the additions are refurbished vintage models of one kind or another.

For more information on the Memphis trolleys, visit www.mata transit.com.

A Taste of New Orleans
Memphis

With so much deep-fried goodness all around, why would you need to visit a Cajun joint in the middle of Tennessee? A few reasons: beignets, alligator bites, muffulettas, and shrimp and grits. And as if the classic Cajun fare alone weren't enough, Beignet Cafe takes its mission seriously, with Creole art adorning the walls and New Orleans Saints paraphernalia and Mardi Gras beads scattered about the establishment.

If you don't have time to head all the way to New Orleans for dinner, Beignet is the next best thing. But dessert is where the cafe really hits home: Obviously, an order of the signature beignets (complete with cherry filling, chocolate syrup, and whipped cream) is a must, but you'll also be tempted by the bread pudding, mark my words, and whichever type of cheesecake tops the menu at the time. The cafe also boasts free Wi-Fi, which still is more rare than as ubiquitous as it should be in Memphis, as well as live music Friday and Saturday nights and a stellar jazz brunch on Sundays, true Naw'lins style.

Beignet Cafe is located at 124 East G. E. Patterson Ave. in Memphis's South Main district. For more information, call (901) 527-1551 or visit www.beignetcafe-memphis.com.

Distressed Denim
Memphis

If you locate this hard-to-find, out-of-the-way warehouse on your own, you deserve a gold star. Situated on the northern outskirts of downtown Memphis in the former Greyhound building that still bears the logo, there's no visible clue that Thigh High Jeans occupies the corridor at the very back of the top floor. And even if you do find it, there's a good chance no one will be home, as they're only open a couple days a week (call ahead). Still, if you do manage to both find it and visit while someone's there, you'll discover a trove of treasures: a collection of denim wear that has been loved and recycled and reconstructed for new owners.

A pair of local artists, photographer Ann Smithwick and painter Kerry Peeples, are the brains behind the operation; they joined together to use their creative talents for an eco-friendly line of remade jeans. But these aren't just any old jeans—they're jeans with morals and a philosophy. Each one is branded with a different saying, quote, or verse from the likes of Shakespeare, Gandhi, and sometimes even the Bible. It's a grab bag of sorts, though: When you place an order, you never know what your new duds might say. Kerry and Ann do, however, provide you with a short questionnaire first to pinpoint your personality type and have an uncanny knack for hitting the nail on the head.

And while you could easily pay $200 for a pair of mass-produced luxury jeans from a department store, at Thigh High you'll fork over a cool $50, as part of the owners' philosophy is giving back and providing customers with premium denim that's also affordable. You can also donate your old jeans to the company by dropping them off directly or at one of the receptacles around town, like Otherlands and other participating coffee shops, or send in a pair and pay for them to be spruced up with a saying (though the owners reiterate that you trust them to pick what your refurbished jeans will say, claiming "it's like getting a fortune cookie").

Everything the duo uses is recycled, right down to the thrifted material and tags made from wildflower seed packets (so you can plant the fruits of their labor once the jeans are in your possession). Best of all: They plan to donate half of their proceeds to a range of local, national, and international philanthropies. How's that for socially conscious fashion with a purpose?

While Thigh High (which gets its name from the giddy high Ann and Kerry hope you get while wearing them) products are not yet available at local retailers, you can e-mail thighhighjeans@gmail .com to make an appointment or visit the online store at www.thigh highjeans.com. The shop carries lines for children, men, and women, including moms, both those expecting and those who already have young 'uns and aren't into the low-rise kinds the kids are wearing these days.

A Brew for Your Thoughts
Memphis

Tennessee may be best known for its whiskey, but it also serves up some damn good beer—with a side of sugary sweet Southern hospitality. Ghost River Brewing, just a smidge over two years old, is already wildly popular with Tennesseans, and it abides by the philosophy that "great water makes great beer," claiming Memphis is home to some of the greatest drinking water on earth (which, I learned, does not come from the Mississippi River, contrary to popular belief; rather, the water for the beer hails from the Ghost River's wetlands).

★ ☆ ★ ☆ ★ ☆ ★ ☆ ★ ☆ ★ ☆ ★ ☆ ★ ☆ ★ ☆ ★ ☆ ★ ☆ ★ ☆ ★ ☆ ★ ☆ ★ ☆ ★ ☆ ★ ☆ ★ ☆ ★ ☆ ★

The people behind Ghost River Brewing, housed in a converted meatpacking plant downtown, want you to enjoy what the brand is all about, generously dispensing six-ounce pours of various brews for you to sample as you learn about the process. The three beers currently produced are the Golden, Glacial Pale Ale, and Brown Ale; there's also a seasonal beer that changes, well, by the season. And it's a company with a cause, too: A portion of all sales goes to the Wolf River Conservancy, a Memphis-based land trust that has helped protect more than 18,000 acres along the Wolf River, from which the Ghost River branches.

Public tours of the brewery are free and held every Saturday at 1:00 p.m. Reservations are required, and be sure to eat before you go—after all the beer you'll no doubt be sampling, your stomach will thank you. Ghost River is served at many bars around town; if you want to take some home to dad, though, you'll have to purchase it (in keg or growler form) from the dock, as it's yet to be sold at the local grocery stores.

Ghost River Brewing is located at 827 South Main St. For more information, call (901) 278-0087 or visit www.ghostriverbrewing.com.

Kitscherama Central

Memphis

Beale Street may be best known for being an all-night party, but it's also decorated with curiosity shops galore. Take A. Schwab, for example. A dry goods store, you'll find everything under the sun just short of the kitchen sink scattered haphazardly among its three levels (one of which is a museum). Jinx-removing oil? A. Schwab has got it. Elvis kitsch? Would you prefer the King's style of glasses (complete with sideburns) or a copy of his driver's license? Suspenders? Sure thing—there are nearly fifty different kinds. Bongo drums, corncob pipes, crystal balls, aged petticoats? All that and much, much, much more. On the second floor, be sure to check out the well-stocked Beale Street Museum, which is a hodgepodge of objects representing Memphis's past.

Beale Street is littered with bustling live music joints, touristy stops, and curiosity stores by the dozen.

A. Schwab is the only remaining original Beale Street establishment, with roots dating back to 1876. The store's cheeky motto is "If you can't get it at A. Schwab, you're probably better off without it!" I'd have to say, that bold statement is alarmingly correct. A. Schwab is located at 163 Beale St. For more information, call (901) 523-9782.

A few doors down, Spencer's meets rock 'n' roll at Tater Red's. Boasting a plethora of skull-themed apparel, Tater has plenty of vintage music posters and Ed Hardy apparel on hand. It's also a great place to snag musician-related kitsch, such as blues stars bobble-head dolls, an autographed and framed U2 photo, electric guitars branded by such musicians as Scotty Moore and Dwight Yoakam, and old-school album covers. Like elsewhere around town, the shop isn't short on voodoo and mojo-related paraphernalia either, so buy your charms or reagents in bulk. Tater Red's is located at 153 Beale St. For more information, call (901) 578-7234 or visit www.taterreds.com.

Still looking for iconic Memphis souvenirs? How about a retro shirt and a bottle of BBQ rub from the shop at BB King's Blues Club at the end of the row? Or a bit of swingin' jazz while you chow down on a rack of ribs? You're in luck because BB King's is a restaurant, gift shop, and blues joint all rolled into one—and you simply can't beat that. BB King's is located at 143 Beale St. For more information, call (901) 524-5464 or visit memphis.bbkingclubs.com.

Bust Out Your Fat Pants

Memphis

With so much fine (read *deep-fried*) Southern food served up regularly, those visiting Memphis on a diet will not fare well. Particularly if visiting in mid-May during the annual World Championship Barbecue-Cooking Contest, alternately referred to as "the Super Bowl of Swine." More than 200 teams cook up some wacky names—past favorites include The Hogfather, Wasted and Basted, and Notorious P.I.G.—as well as some inventive flavors and combinations in an attempt to impress world-class tasters judging their concoctions at Tom Lee Park. Over $90,000 in prizes are awarded each year.

For those who'd rather judge than be judged, you'll find your calling in the People's Choice tent, where you can tantalize your taste buds by sampling an array of la crème de la crème in barbecue (you'll be asked to purchase a sample kit for a nominal fee). The Cooker Caravan is a good place to learn the ropes, as you'll get a glimpse into the methods of some serious pros and be given a tour of the premises (they depart every half hour). Just don't neglect to stick around for the Ms. Piggie pageant, where grown men don tutus and snouts and their lady friends kick up their heels and oink in approval.

The barbecue fest is part of the much revered Memphis in May International Festival, which also comprises the Beale Street Music

Festival, a sunset symphony in the park, and various other cultural events, such as live music performances, artisans of all crafts and trades, and motivational speakers. For more information, log onto www.memphisinmay.org.

A House with a History

Memphis

There's nary an establishment in all of Memphis that contains nearly as much history as the Hunt-Phelan House does. Built in 1828 and then purchased by Eli and Julia Driver in 1850, the house has been passed down from generation to generation—but always to male heirs (if there wasn't one, it went to the daughter's husband). The home was once a vital stop on the Underground Railroad.

Between 1863 and 1865 the home was used as a hospital for wounded soldiers; Union general Ulysses S. Grant used the house as his headquarters for a short time and planned the Siege of Vicksburg from the library. After the war ended, the family petitioned the U.S. government for the return of their home, and President Andrew Johnson granted this request; years of repairs to reverse the war damage followed. In the second half of the twentieth century, the reclusive Stephen Rice Phelan inherited the property. After he died in the early 1990s, his nephew Bill Day assumed ownership and undertook the massive task of renovating the home.

Phelan was a quirky man in his old age, and had the antebellum mansion chained and padlocked, the exterior almost completely masked by tall grass and weeds. The inside was stacked high with all sorts of belongings—grocery lists, dental records, and the like—from the old home's many inhabitants throughout the decades, as well as furniture custom made in France and still wrapped in newspaper from its journey across the sea. Day took it upon himself to make the house into the grand relic it once was. After sorting through everything, he sold the majority of artifacts to fund the more than $1 million of renovations and transformation of the house into a nonprofit

Built more than 180 years ago, the Hunt-Phelan House now serves as the city's finest inn.

organization, museum, and, later, a luxury inn. It's stint as a museum was unsuccessful and brief before it found its calling in hospitality.

Many features of the historic home remain from the original structure, such as the soaring doors, chandeliers, and floors (check out the scuff marks on the staircases from the soldiers' spurs). The mansion houses a total of sixteen rooms on five acres and rents ten suites to guests (five of which are housed in an annex next door). Murals adorn many of the walls in the rooms in the main house and were added by a group of local art students during the renovation period to reflect the home in its heyday. New bathrooms and modern amenities have been added throughout the premises to make it truly the nicest place to lay your head in all of Memphis, if not the whole of Tennessee.

The Inn at Hunt-Phelan is located at 533 Beale St. For more information, call (901) 525-8225 or visit www.huntphelan.com. The inn also lays claim to one of the finest restaurants around, having garnered four stars and various dining accolades, and an incredibly well-stocked bar.

Oink, Oink
Memphis

If pickled pigs feet chased by "a 40" (a forty-ounce cold brew) doesn't sound like a delicacy worth tryin', then you haven't been in the South long enough, my friend. A hole-in-the-wall blues joint, Wild Bill's is as eccentric as its name might suggest. People of all ages, skin color, and origin meet to get down to the club's soulful blues, pumped out on command by a house band.

This place ain't fancy: It's a true neighborhood juke joint where beer and malt liquor are served only in forty-ounce bottles. The band fills much of the dance floor, but there are still slivers of space where you can get out and shake your moneymaker (and, honey, you better—this isn't a stop for wallflowers). A bonus: It's not located on Beale Street, so those who want to venture far from the maddening crowd have an alternative. Don't be fooled, though—tourists have caught wind of this nondescript yet happening hot spot, so it's no longer the locals-only place it once was.

Wild Bill's is located at 1580 Vollintine Ave. For more information, call (901) 726-5473.

A Cup of Joe
Memphis

In most big American cities, if you want your daily brew, you're going to have to cave and get it at Starbuck's, Peet's, Tully's, or another national chain with such a ubiquitous presence. In Memphis, you'll find the 'bux, but you'll also be pleased to see that the local fair-trade

Ugly Mug Coffee, a Memphis brand with attitude to spare, is available at many local grocery stores such as Schnuck's.

coffee Ugly Mug is nearly as prevalent, not to mention every bit as tasty.

And it's a brand with attitude, too. The playful personality is displayed in all of the marketing and promotional material, as well as on each bag of coffee, which not only pictures bleary-eyed people clearly in need of a cup or ten, but also catchy phrases like "Oh, what a beautiful morning" and "You are now leaving Sleepy-Town." Past ads have boasted such sayings as "You can't get a restraining order for the sun. It comes and goes as it pleases, a gaseous, unwelcome Peeping Tom peeking in between the blinds." Or "The snooze button is a pusher. Selling heaven in seven-minute increments." The whole tongue-in-cheek concept is, in one word, genius. Brews are aptly named, too, such as Hardy Passion, Making Waves, and Saving Grace.

Ugly Mug Coffee started out in a church basement and has now reached regional fame; the company continues to grow in its faith-based and philanthropic relations, its president says. The coffee beans are grown in Brazil, Colombia, Ethiopia, Guatemala, Costa Rica, Mexico, Nicaragua, Indonesia, and Peru. Many locals say the best place to stock up on Ugly Mug is at the midtown Schnuck's (a local grocery chain) on Union Avenue. Aside from your basic brews, you'll find other delectable varieties like ground Southern Pecan, Spiced Chai, and Crème Brulee Hot Chocolate.

For more information, to order online, or to find locations that sell Ugly Mug, visit www.uglymugcoffee.com.

Ahoy, Matey!
Memphis

As if it weren't enough to have one pirate-themed bar, Memphis boasts two. At Buccaneer downtown, a pirate wielding a wooden spoon and a fishnet by the entrance will give you a taste of what you're in for as you approach the ramshackle bungalow (as if the name alone didn't quite tip you off). Live music is particularly popular here—the Bucc (as it's dubbed by regulars) stands at the forefront

51

★ ★

of Memphis's underground music and indie scene—though the local magazine calls it "more of a dinghy than a pirate ship," based on its size.

Buccaneer is located at 1368 Monroe Ave. For more information, call (901) 278-0909.

To be honest, I can't quite figure the second one out. The Cove, a midtown watering hole with a bare facade, is filled to the brim with pirate-y goodness inside, yet it serves carefully prepared, totally unrelated cocktails like the Vampire, a creative spin on the Bloody Mary comprising tequila, tomato juice, red chili salt, and balsamic vinegar. It also prides itself on its jazzy New Orleans style—it serves the world-famous Café du Monde coffee, as well as a pre–Civil War concoction, the Sazerac, which dates back to 1793 and uses both rye whiskey and absinthe—while extending the nautical theme to encompass a mast over the bar and a mural of sailors. Its specialty dish is oysters on the half-shell (just like Jack Sparrow liked them, right?); the bar also airs cult classic movies on rotation and hosts live jazz, bluegrass, and folk groups.

The Cove is located at 2559 Broad Ave. in Memphis. For more information, call (901) 730-0719 or check out www.thecovememphis .com.

Here Comes the Sun
Memphis

Ground zero for the rock 'n' roll industry, Sun Studio has been responsible for launching many a musician's career, and many a musician you know, too. Elvis Presley, Johnny Cash, and Jerry Lee Lewis ring a bell? And it was all due to a twenty-seven-year-old man who grew up on a farm and took a total gamble on an industry that laid dormant at the time.

In 1950 Alabama-born Sam Phillips opened Memphis Recording Service at 706 Union Ave., where he also launched his own label, Sun Records, two years later. He recorded everything from musical performances to weddings and funerals and sold them all. He catered to amateurs, giving them a chance in the spotlight and drawing the likes of B. B. King. In 1953 Elvis Presley walked into the studio to record a disc for his mother for her birthday. The rest is history.

Phillips went on to become one of the most successful music producers of all time, his repertoire of talent spanning everything from rock to blues to country, and the brains behind the Million Dollar Quartet (Elvis, Cash, Lewis, and Carl Perkins). In 1955 he went one step further and started a radio station, WHER, which became the first all-girl radio station in the nation, as only women worked in its office. Phillips was one of the first inductees into the Rock and Roll Hall of Fame and the first nonperformer to be recognized by the Rockabilly Hall of Fame. He also holds a spot in the Alabama Music Hall of Fame, the Country Music Hall of Fame, and the Blues Hall of Fame. That's a whole lot of fame for one farm boy from the Tennessee-Alabama border!

Sun Studio is still located at its original Union Avenue home in downtown Memphis, just a quick drive from Beale Street. Tours are given daily at the bottom half of every hour for a fee and last roughly an hour and a half. There's a free shuttle that travels to and from Sun Studio, Graceland, and the Rock 'n' Soul Museum. Sun also releases regular studio-session podcasts on both YouTube and public television. For more information, call (800) 441-6249 or visit www.sun studio.com.

Step Right Up
Memphis

Let's be honest: You don't go to the carnival for the rides. Nor do you go for the games, rigged so you go home without a prize to show for your efforts, your pockets significantly lighter. You go to the carnival for one reason and one reason only: the food.

Lynette and Eldrid Hill recognized this fact and came up with the million-dollar idea—to open a restaurant that serves carnival food

★ ★

This themed eatery features the best in carnival fare—from corn dogs to funnel cakes, it offers artery-clogging delights galore.

every day. The Hills already had a trailer that sold such fare and would make appearances at festivals and flea markets. Eldrid also had a background in the food industry, having worked for Elvis's cousin running his restaurant for years. So when the fair permanently left Memphis, they devised a way to keep it around—at least in spirit—all day, every day, by opening a storefront.

The menu at Carnival Food has everything you could possibly dream up: Philly cheesesteak, nachos, funnel cakes (with various toppings such as powdered sugar, chocolate, strawberries, whipped cream, and ice cream), hot wings, corn dogs, cotton candy, snow cones, popcorn, burgers, BBQ sandwiches, catfish, bratwurst, fries, turkey legs, ice cream, and much more. (A word to the wise: Don't plan on eating here if you have any sort of heart condition.) In keeping with the theme, the restaurant also has board games (like Monopoly and dominos), arcade games, and miniature basketball hoops. The Hills still have a booth selling a similar, but limited, menu at the Third Avenue flea market on Saturdays.

Carnival Food is located at 2235 Covington Pike, Suite 9, in a former Mexican restaurant in a strip mall. For more information, call (901) 377-0089 or visit www.carnival.food.officelive.com.

Praise the Lord!
Memphis

Best known for crooning such hits such as "Let's Stay Together," Al Green found Jesus long after he'd risen to stardom, when his girlfriend at the time committed suicide in his Memphis home in 1974. After he refused to marry her, Mary Woodson White attacked him with a pan of boiling grits, giving him third-degree burns all over his body, before she took her own life.

According to Green, who had a Billboard Top 100 hit at the time, this incident was just the wake-up call he needed. He sought out religion to change his life and, just two years later, became an ordained pastor at Full Gospel Tabernacle Church, where he continues to preach to this day. His Pentecostal services are visited by the masses, particularly by those starstruck by Al Green the Musician rather than Al Green the Reverend (though there are quite a few of the latter as well).

Services begin around 11:00 a.m. every Sunday and are open to all. But Green is not always on hand to preach; sometimes a deacon stands in for him. The only day of the year you're assured of his presence is Easter Sunday. And don't be that tacky tourist who tries to snap photos during the service if he does happen to show; you won't make any friends that way. Nor will you win over Reverend Green by being stingy when it's time to tithe; instead of passing a collection plate around, he has the whole congregation come up front in a very unorthodox manner and has been known to shame those—if only with a glance of the eye—who give anything less than $20. Whether or not you have the pleasure of seeing Green preach, there will be plenty of the Pentecostal shenanigans you may have heard about but never seen in the flesh—speaking in tongues, falling to the floor in an epileptic fit—and a whole lotta gospel.

Full Gospel Tabernacle is located at 787 Hale Rd. in Memphis. For more information, call (901) 396-9192.

Dawn of the Dead
Memphis

If ever there were a more perfect setting for a serene, yet slightly spooky, movie scene in a cemetery, it would be at Elmwood. Established as part of the rural cemetery movement of the nineteenth century, the eighty acres of beautiful sprawling real estate with shady groves and sweeping vistas comprise one of Memphis's loveliest areas, despite its ominous aura.

Elmwood is the final resting place of roughly half of the victims of the city's widespread 1878 yellow fever epidemic, an outbreak that infected 20,000 people along the Mississippi River and claimed 5,000 lives, and is a great spot for reflection and for paying your respects. More than 1,000 Confederate soldiers and veterans were laid to rest here, as well as those who fought in the Revolutionary War and just about every war since. In 2002 the cemetery was placed on the National Register of Historic Places. Take a stroll through the grounds and admire the many towering monuments, statues, and mausoleums.

Elmwood Cemetery is located at 824 South Dudley St. in East Memphis. For more information, call (901) 774-3212 or visit www .elmwoodcemetery.org. Docent-led tours are scheduled every Saturday at 10:30 a.m. They last an hour and a fee is charged. Group tours are also available during the week for groups of ten or more adults.

★ ★

The Film Guru
Memphis

He may have a Sundance Film Festival award to his name, not to mention an Academy Award for Best Original Song from one of his movies, but that hasn't stopped Craig Brewer from sticking to his roots. The screenwriter and director writes what he knows, and what he knows is Memphis.

Brewer's biggest films, *Hustle & Flow* (the Oscar winner) and *Black Snake Moan,* not only were based in Memphis, but filmed here as well; both are good introductions to the city before you visit. Taking his love for this city to an extreme, Craig even wrote a short-lived MTV series, *5 Dollar Cover,* that took place in Memphis and followed

Local Yokels

Craig Brewer and the aforementioned musicians aside, here is a very small selection of past and present stars who proudly hail from Memphis:

Justin Timberlake, musician

Ginnifer Goodwin, actress

Cybill Shepherd, actress

Judge Joe Brown, politician

Kathy Bates, actress

Tennessee Williams, playwright

Dixie Carter, actress

Shelby Foote, author

Morgan Freeman, actor

Aretha Franklin, singer

Pat and Gina Neely, celebrity chefs

Reggie White, NFL player

Rick Dees, disc jockey

Shannen Doherty, actress

★ ★

a group of local musicians—their professional, personal and love lives—as they vied to make names for themselves. The series has since expanded to other cities.

Strummin' and Pickin'
Memphis

Even if you're not a guitar fanatic, you've no doubt heard of Gibson, the most well-known supplier of the stringed instrument in the world. Well, next time you're in Memphis, you can stop by the headquarters and see just how the carved pieces of tonewood are made, the company's specialty being the semi-hollow body. On your docent-led tour, you'll see original models played by the likes of Pete Townsend, Eric Clapton, B. B. King, and, of course, Elvis. (Are you sensing a theme? There's nothing you can do to escape the King in this town.) You'll see the rims and panels being shaped, and the finished product painted and buffed.

The Gibson Guitar Factory is located at 145 Lt. George W. Lee Ave. in downtown Memphis. For more information, call (800) 987-9852.

What Do Snow Cones and a Car Wash Have in Common?
Memphis

Not much, actually, other than the fact that Memphis's most popular snow cone spot, Jerry's Sno-Cones and Car Wash, incorporates both themes. If you didn't have your fill of junk at Carnival Food, head on down to Jerry's, a long-standing establishment that was featured in the film *Great Balls of Fire*, for sweet satisfaction.

From the outside, Jerry's pink and green facade looks like a small-town ice-cream parlor, but in reality it serves up hundreds of flavors of shaved ice. (They do, however, offer soft-serve cones and cups for the traditionalist.) Some loyal patrons attribute Jerry's greatness to the fact that the cones manage to pull off the consistency of actual snow, not ice. You'll find regular ol' flavors like cherry, coconut, and blue raspberry mingling with more interesting concoctions like wedding cake, a fan favorite that allegedly tastes just like the real thing. If you order your cone "supreme," you'll find a nice surprise: a few layers of vanilla soft-serve added to your snow.

The establishment was recently taken over by new owners, who added actual food to the menu as well. To be clear, Jerry's is takeout only, and the line is often what seems like a mile long. Bear in mind, too, that it accepts cash only.

Jerry's is located at 1657 Wells Station Rd. in Memphis. For more information, call (901) 767-2659.

Put Your Records On
Memphis

Old-fashioned record stores are a dying breed. If you manage to locate one, it probably has a well-stocked CD section with one shelf dedicated to the archaic record. Well, not Goner. Not only does the one-stop music shop stock LPs and 45s, they'll buy your aging models

One of a very few old-school record stores, Goner has a better selection than you'll find anywhere, stocking everything from LPs and 45s to CDs.

as well and resale them in the store, alongside new and/or rare CDs and vinyl.

With an emphasis on heavy metal, blues, punk, and soul, Goner's expansive collection is a bit overwhelming, to say the least. You can even listen to albums before you close the deal and purchase them—how's that for customer service? Prices are extremely affordable given the merchandise, and you can place your orders over the phone or the Web, too, should you not be available to visit in person. The shop also has its own eponymous label, which is responsible for Goner-fest, the four-day music extravaganza that consumes Memphis each September.

Goner Records is located at 2152 Young Ave. in Memphis's Cooper-Young district. For more information, call (901) 722-0095 or visit www.goner-records.com.

A Coffee Shop with Attitude
Memphis

From the outside, it looks like a bunch of hippies sporting tie-dye might be inside lighting up a bong, with the smell of incense permeating the air. Hardly. On the inside, you'll find writers and artists and musicians and those simply just wanting to enjoy a cup of joe in the cozy confines of Otherlands.

Otherlands is a hip and spacious coffee bar with a menu of delightful food and caffeinated beverages galore. (The fresh ginger snap tea is a personal favorite.) The free Wi-Fi (not to mention walls of open power outlets, a rarity in most coffee shops) made it an instant destination for the laptop set, ensuring that the seats stay warm and the house is always packed. Live music gigs on weekend nights mean that the crowds never abate. Additionally, the gift shop—well stocked with toys, trinkets, cards, incense, and "exotic gifts"—is worthy of a gander.

Otherlands is located at 641 South Cooper St. in Memphis' Cooper-Young district. For more information, call (901) 278-4994 or visit www.otherlandscoffeebar.com.

A caffeine-infused haven for midtown Memphians, Otherlands is a great spot to grab a bite while surfing the Web (for free) or catching up with a pal over a spot of tea.

Not Your Mama's Neighborhood Deli

Memphis

If you're looking for cold cuts and gourmet cheese, Young Avenue Deli is not the place for you. Sure, it's got food—more of the battered-and-fried, smothered-and-covered variety—but music and nightlife are more this midtown Memphis spot's forte. You'll find hippies, punk rockers, hipsters, college kids, and old dudes all convening in this one common indie hot spot for a beer and a bit of live music.

Though if you like a good fry—and who doesn't?—you'll want to order a batch of frites (and maybe a side of deep-fried artichoke hearts while you're at it); *USA Today* bestowed the honor of "Top Ten Fries in the Nation" upon Young Avenue. There's also a decent vegetarian selection, something uncommon in the South, as well as a stellar beer menu. This place is so hopping that table service, both food and booze, is usually slooooow (and oftentimes aloof), and there's often a sizable line out front, so diners should arrive well before peak meal and bar times. Consider yourself forewarned.

Young Avenue Deli is located at 2119 Young Ave. in Memphis's Cooper-Young district. There is a cover charge for band nights. For prices and more information, visit www.youngavenuedeli.com or call (901) 278-0034.

Pamper Yourself
Memphis

With a name like Beauty Shop, you might expect a visit to this Cooper-Young establishment to consist of a cut and color. Well, maybe at one point—the place was originally a beauty parlor after all, hence the name—but today it's one of midtown Memphis's more popular lunch spots. And with daily grilled cheese, soup, and ravioli specials, as well as a menu chock-full of artisan sandwiches and salads with unique spreads like Sriracha mayo or mint jelly, what's not to love?

Just take my advice and save room for dessert: With gelato and floats in every flavor imaginable, you'll want a sweet treat to top off your meal (I recommend the cinnamon milk shake or coconut sorbet). Traces of the beauty parlor days of yore remain: For example, many of the seats rest against old-fashioned hair dryers.

Beauty Shop is located at 966 South Cooper in Memphis's Cooper-Young district. For more information, call (901) 272-7111 or visit www.thebeautyshoprestaurant.com.

This trendy Cooper-Young restaurant channels an old-fashioned beauty parlor—and indeed it once was.

Studio 54

Memphis

This place is unassuming in its out-of-the-way location (somewhere between the trendy South Main district and the historic Lorraine Motel) and its borderline sketchy facade. But that doesn't stop Hollywood Disco—formerly and often referred to interchangeably as Raiford's—from being the place to go to exercise your dancing shoes.

As if the soulful tunes of the '60s and '70s that the place blares out over the loudspeaker weren't enough of a draw, how about the fact

One of Memphis's remaining authentic discos, this nightlife hot spot will transport you back to 1977.

that it's a costume party on a nightly basis? From pimp suits to sailor getups to Afros, you'll find it all out on the red glow of the dance floor. Hollywood Disco is not for the easily rattled either: The stripper pole in the corner gets a lot of use from patrons, men and women alike.

While still wildly popular today, Hollywood Disco was once the greatest club in all of West Tennessee, so squint your eyes and, through your beer goggles, view the night as a history lesson and try to see it as it once was.

Hollywood Disco is located at 115 Vance Ave. in downtown Memphis. For more information, call (901) 528-9313 or visit www.hollywood disco.com.

Pigskin & Fame

In 2009 a locally well-known Memphis family was launched to international fame thanks to a little movie called **The Blind Side,** which opened to much acclaim and helped Sandra Bullock claim her first Oscar for the role of housewife Leigh Anne Tuohy.

If you didn't catch the film, here's a synopsis: A well-to-do family who made their fortune in the fast-food industry—Taco Bell and Long John Silver's, among others—adopts a troubled boy, Michael Oher, from a rough area and gives him a chance, turning him into one of the biggest football stars Memphis has ever seen. Out of loyalty to the family, he goes on to be a collegiate star at Ole Miss, the Tuohys' alma mater, before going pro and signing to the Baltimore Ravens as a first-round pick.

It's a touching tale of love, faith, and togetherness that's remarkably representative of the South and its people. While the movie was completely shot in Georgia, it all takes place in Memphis. Check out the book upon which the movie was based, *The Blind Side: Evolution of a Game,* or the flick itself to learn more about one of Memphis's most iconic twenty-first-century families.

Good for the Soul

Memphis

Once a favorite haunt of Martin Luther King Jr., the Four Way Grill has been hopping since it opened in 1946. Other luminaries like Don King and B. B. King were frequent diners as well; you'll find their photos decorating the walls of the establishment.

One of the joints that define Memphis as "Soulsville, USA," the Four Way is located in what was once an all-black neighborhood and has long been named the city's "Best Soul Food" in just about every publication this side of the Mississippi. Juicy fried green tomatoes, tart black-eyed peas, squishy cornbread, chewy pork chops, and melt-in-your-mouth sweet potato pie are just a few of the mouthwatering delicacies that top the menu—don't be afraid to go back for seconds.

The Four Way Grill is located at 998 Mississippi Blvd. in south Memphis. For more information, call (901) 507-1519.

Knuckleheads
Skullbone

With a name like Skullbone, you've got to wonder about the town's origins. And luckily this rough-and-tumble spot, home to just fifty residents, doesn't disappoint: It does, in fact, have a story behind its name.

Founded in 1839, Skullbone was at one time the home to bare-knuckle prizefighting, often referred to as a "fist and skull bone" competition. This style of roughhousing—which was not performed for vengeance, but rather for sport and entertainment—only allowed for blows above the chest and operated under no time limits, so the fighter with the most endurance literally came out on top. This odd contest put Skullbone on the map and was a favorite pastime until early in the twentieth century. Historical accounts and documents claim that Davy Crockett, who roamed these corridors, was a frequent participant.

But the quirkiness of the town encompasses more than just its knuckleheads. Originally thought to be a habitat of Chickasaw Indians, in its earlier days—the 1800s and early 1900s—Skullbone could have given the Wild, Wild West a run for its money, with gang activity, prostitution, and racism (the last of which, sadly, is known to still exist in the area) running rampant in the region. The town was never incorporated, and lawlessness, particularly during the Civil War, was a major problem.

In the 1950s the governor at the time decided to declare an expanse of land between the Tennessee and Mississippi Rivers the "Kingdom of Skullbonia," encompassing a much larger area surrounding the actual village of Skullbone. Later, governor Gordon Browning knocked it down a peg, declaring the area the "Territory of Skullbonia."

Today Skullbone hosts many touring rock bands and summer concerts at Skullbone Music Park. For information on lineups and events, call Allen Blankenship at (731) 742-4291 or visit www.skullbonemusic park.com.

The town's other claim to fame is its Hampton's General Store, which has found its way onto the National Register of Historic Places and is essentially the only remaining element to Skullbonia. It's a popular spot for, you guessed it, skull-and-crossbones types of souvenirs and can be found at the intersection of Trezevant Highway and Shades Bridge Road. The town itself is located about 40 miles north of Jackson, off US 45 East.

Shake, Shake, Shake
Tiptonville

A little-known fact about West Tennessee (even to most West Tennesseans) is that it sits in a high-risk earthquake zone. While tornadoes are common, running rampant through the state's central corridor, earthquakes are far less frequent occurrences despite the seismic activity along the Mississippi River. But this wasn't always the case.

In 1811 and 1812 three of the largest quakes in all of American history struck this area of the country—so hard, in fact, that they even reversed the flow of the Mississippi (albeit temporarily). The New Madrid earthquakes, as they were called, caused a depression east of the river; it began to sink and the river water began filling it up, covering the cypress trees that can still be found on the lakebed. Today Reelfoot Lake is popular with hunters and anglers, as well as those passing through Tennessee who want a taste of the great outdoors.

★ ★ ★ ★ ★ ★ ★ ★ ★ ★★ ★

Whoa, Boy!

Speaking of fishin', don't go pulling any cowboy maneuvers while you're frolicking at Reelfoot. While casting your rod is definitely allowed, catching a fish with a lasso is illegal (lest you have any wiseguy ideas). So leave your chaps, spurs, and noble steed at home, old boy, and stick to fishing the normal way—with a pole or, heck, even your own bare hands.

You'll also find a cluster of lodges and resorts (though don't expect fancy) along the waterfront, should you want to pop over for a night or a bite.

For more information on Reelfoot Lake, log onto www.visitreel footlake.com or call (731) 253-8003.

I'm a Little Teapot

Trenton

Why wouldn't Middle of Nowhere, Tennessee, some 4,000 miles from England, the unofficial international tea headquarters, boast the world's largest teapot collection? And a very specific collection at that, comprising only porcelain Veilleuses-Theieres, or night-light models.

The collection came to Trenton when a native who had relocated to New York decided to get rid of his multimillion-dollar collection, which included more than 500 pieces. His initial instinct was to donate the teapots to New York City's famed Metropolitan Museum of Art, but his brother convinced him to stick to his roots and ship them back to Trenton instead. The teapots span a century's worth of history, from 1750 to 1860.

Until her death in 2006, Evelyn Hardwood doubled as the city recorder and the exhibit's acting curator. Her duties entailed providing group tours and serving as the Teapot Parade Marshal, an honor if there ever was one in Trenton. For the past thirty years, Trenton has furthered the celebration of the teapot, honoring its existence in a weeklong Teapot Festival at the end of April each year. Thanks to teapots putting the city in the public eye, its slogan is "Trenton: A Tea-riffic Town" (ha ha).

Trenton is situated 30 miles north of Jackson off TN 5. The Teapot Collection is located downtown at 309 South College St. For more information on the museum or festival, call (731) 855-2013 or visit www.teapotcollection.com.

Middle Tennessee

2

Middle

Whereas West Tennessee *is flat and monotonous and East Tennessee is rocky and mountainous, Middle Tennessee has a landscape all its own. Composed of rolling green hills and a dominating plateau (the Cumberland), the middle slab of the state is prime tornado territory due to its geography, though many twisters die off when they hit the plateau's boundary before wreaking too much havoc. The region is also one of the most culturally rich and diverse thanks to its cluster of cities, big and small, near its heart.*

The largest and most action-packed—though, oddly, the least densely populated—of the state's three divisions, the central sliver is home to the capital and Tennessee's second-biggest city, Nashville, which lies in its epicenter. Nashville is best known on a global scale for being the home of country music, and it's true—you can't go far without stumbling upon a singer-songwriter, a relative of a famed country musician past or present, or a bustling live music joint. It's what gives Tennessee such character and attitude. But that's not all the region has to offer.

Many of the towns that surround the capital played vital roles in the Civil War, and you'll find many a battlefield, cemetery, and memorial scattered about, particularly in the upscale suburbs of Franklin and Brentwood. Andrew Jackson—former state governor, president, and army general—once ruled these parts, and many of the state's landmarks are named in his honor.

★ ★

It's no big secret that *Nashville* and
country music are synonymous.

Just don't forget to set your clock back when nearing Middle Tennessee's eastern border: Here draws the line between the Central and
Eastern time zones.

The Legend of the Bell Witch

Adams

Whether it's a true tale or parents' ploy to scare the bejesus out of their rugrats remains unknown, but every child in Tennessee starts hearing about the mysterious Bell Witch from a young age. Dating back to 1817, the Bell Witch allegedly is a sinister entity who took it upon herself to haunt a pioneer family in Adams, Tennessee, for the coming decade. But this isn't your average ghost story: A number of the town's residents have attested, via manuscripts and affidavits, to the fact that the Bell Witch really did exist.

The family of note was the Bells, who relocated to Robertson County at the beginning of the nineteenth century. John Bell purchased a large expanse of land for his family to occupy and was out inspecting his corn crops one day when an odd-looking animal with the body of a dog and the head of a rabbit appeared in front of him. He shot at it with his rifle, but it scurried away.

From then on out, mysterious sounds—beatings on the outside of their log cabin, an unidentified voice—became the norm, but the Bells never caught the culprit. The Bell children continued to experience a string of strange encounters, such as unknown scratching on their bedposts, assaults and slappings, and bed covers being pulled off them in the middle of the night. Family friends stayed over in the house and attested to similar occurrences. Over time, a voice was heard, starting as a whisper and growing louder: It would quote scripture, sing hymns, and give sermons. The legend became so widespread that Andrew Jackson, who was a major general at the time, took an interest in the tale, even visiting the farm with his men, who all fell victim to the witch as well.

John Bell began suffering facial seizures as he grew older, which often rendered him speechless. In 1820 he fell into a coma and died the following day; a vial of some strange liquid that he was said to have ingested was found near his body. No one knew where it came from, but when it was force-fed to the family cat, the feline also perished. The Bell Witch's voice was heard saying she fed it to John; she also spoke and sang at the graveyard while he was buried and later told John's wife, Lucy, that she would return in seven years. She kept her word and came back to haunt John Jr.

People in Adams still say they hear rumblings of the Bell Witch from time to time, so keep your ears alert and see if she speaks to you. Adams is located 40 miles northwest of Nashville. To get there, take I-24 west, then TN 256 north.

Ostrich Burgers, RC Cola, and MoonPies, Oh My!

Bell Buckle

A mere blip on the map just southeast of Franklin en route to Shelbyville—and a mecca for the internationally celebrated Tennessee walking horse—Bell Buckle is known for two things: RC Cola and MoonPies. Wait, make that three. Aside from the annual summer fest celebrating the origins of the aforementioned indulgences, the only other thing drawing people to this Podunk is its famed cafe.

Don't know what a meat-and-three is? Well, then clearly you can't call yourself a true Southerner. If you want to taste la crème de la crème of the classic home-cooked meat dish and three sides, there's no better place to start. And with ostrich burgers one pièce de résistance—you'll see the feathered friends at their home on a farm leading into the town—and a steaming plate of biscuits and gravy to gulp down afterward, what's not to love? Just don't pass on the pie. In Tennessee, there's always pie.

The cafe was formerly a notable music studio, Bell Buckle Records, where some of the great country music artists got their starts. Vinyl, slipcovers, autographed glossies, and other related musical bric-a-brac wallpaper the interior. Every Friday and Saturday evening, the cafe offers live music with no admission charge, and Thursday is songwriters' night.

Bell Buckle Cafe is located at 16 Railroad Square in the town of the same name. Bell Buckle is 20 miles south of Murfreesboro. To

★ ★

A Wealth of Nations

Think the stereotype of Tennesseans being uncultured and untraveled is true? Think again. Many of us have ventured outside to see the world, but others just plain don't see a need to leave when we have such cities as Milan, Denmark, Athens, Lebanon, and Rome within our state's confines. (Either that, or each city's founders were lacking in the creativity department when giving name to their claim.)

get there, take US 231 south, then go left at Madison Street once you reach the town. Take another left on Railroad Street to arrive in the town square where the cafe is located. For more information, call (931) 389-9693 or visit www.bellbucklecafe.com.

A Watering Hole

Beersheba Springs

While Beersheba Porter Cain was out for a leisurely stroll one day in 1833, little did she know she would stumble upon something that would not only make her a household name in Tennessee, but also put her down in the history books. For what she found was a chalybeate (iron salts) spring perched high above the Collins River Valley.

This little oasis, named Beersheba Springs for its founder, quickly became the place to see and be seen in the nineteenth century. By 1836 it was a booming resort town with a majestic hotel; as it grew, more and more slaves were brought in to tend to the antebellum property. Then the Civil War ravaged the area, and those at

★ ★

Beersheba could only watch in shock and terror at the battles taking place below from the wooden observatory at the front of the hotel. Once fighting ceased, the resort fell into the hands of Yankees and was closed for a stint. When it reopened in 1870, it never quite found its footing again. Today it's used for retreats, assemblies, and summer camps.

You can still take a peek at the original edifice (owned by the Methodist Assembly) by driving by 524 Armfield Ave. You can also visit the stately old place during the Beersheba Springs Arts & Crafts Fair, which has welcomed quite a bit of talent in its fifty years of existence and is generally celebrated the weekend before Labor Day. For more information, call (931) 692-3733.

Beersheba Springs is located about 20 miles east of I-24. Leave the interstate at exit 127 near Pelham, then follow TN 50 east for 15 miles before turning left onto TN 56 and continuing north into the town.

Hee Haw
Bethel

One of Tennessee's most charming attributes is, without a doubt, its small-town traditions, particularly ones that occur with such frequency and fervor as Bethel's Pickin' and Grinnin', which takes place every month at the community center.

Burgers and dogs are cooked up on the grill and generously doled out by the friendliest of neighbors. A covered pavilion serves as the stage, where those feeling jolly can kick up their heels and join in the festivities. A talented repertoire of gospel singers and bluegrass players is often on hand to get the evening started out right. The shindig kicks off at 7:00 p.m. the third Saturday of each month.

Bethel Community Center is located at 4357 Skelley Rd. in Bethel, just south of Leiper's Fork. For more information, visit www.bethel communitycenter.com.

I've Been Workin' on the Railroad

Chapel Hill

As "The Legend of the Bell Witch" entry demonstrated, Tennessee has no lack of alleged paranormal activity. But one of the spookiest tales does not involve a spiteful witch, but rather the most well-known ghost lights around.

Long ago, a signalman working for the train system was killed one particularly stormy night. His job was to walk atop the cars and inspect the brakes on each one. He always carried with him a bright beam of light to guide his way, a lantern that could be seen for miles and miles, but that fateful evening he fell on the slippery tracks. You can imagine what happened next: He was hit by a train and decapitated. His head was never found, though his body was.

Many people passing through Chapel Hill have claimed to have seen the vague outline of lantern lights in the distance, only when they got closer, nothing—or no one—was there. The old signalman is said to still wander these parts searching for his lost head. And no matter where you go in Tennessee, you'll meet somebody who knows somebody who has seen the ghostly lights from Chapel Hill.

A Whistlestop Cafe

Christiana

True, back in the day, Miller's Grocery might not have been anything special when bustling country stores were a dime a dozen. But today, in modern times, that's exactly what makes it unique—it's a former country store (and still poses under that guise) that has been one of the area's best-kept secrets since it was transformed into a cafe and antiques store in 1995.

The town of Christiana is so small it doesn't even have a stoplight to its name, yet that doesn't keep those hankerin' for some fine Southern cuisine from driving from all over the state to this little hot pocket of home-cooked cuisine, particularly for the weekly Sunday buffet, which many say is like a trip to Grandma's house with all the

cousins and extended family present for the occasion. And the kitchen staff at Miller's claims they never know exactly what will be on that buffet until the night before or sometimes even the morning of—but you better believe it will be good. On Friday and Saturday nights, you'll experience a sampling of bluegrass, folk, and Americana music.

Miller's Grocery is located at 7011 Main St. in Christiana. For more information, call (615) 893-1878 or visit www.millersgrocery.com.

School Days, Mule Days
Columbia

Let's be up front: A mule is not a horse. Nor is it a donkey. A mule is its own breed and a combination of the two: an offspring of a male donkey and a female horse. Got it? Good. Now, you're free to go on your merry way and enjoy Mule Day to the fullest.

Each April, Columbia becomes a cacophony of "nayyyys" when hundreds of 1,000-pound equines descend upon its downtown. A well-known tradition since 1840, Mule Day originally was a celebrated Monday each year when breeders brought their livestock to show; it was one of the largest livestock markets in the world. Today it's not uncommon for upward of 200,000 people to come marvel at the spectacle, which has morphed into a four-day event, chock-full of Appalachian street food carts, music, square dancing, and arts and crafts. Additionally, there's gospel music, church services, pool tournaments, chili suppers, and one of the South's favorite pastimes, clogging.

Competitions include "working mule" and "best of breed" (sorry, open only to the mules), Mule Day Queen (open only to the *Homo sapiens*), mule driving, and a mule pull. Since 1934 one of the highlights of the event has been the Mule Day Festival, held on a Saturday, with the best floats and entries receiving ribbons and prize money.

For more information on Mule Day, call the headquarters at (931) 381-9557 or visit www.muleday.net.

Bigfoot Lives Here
Dodson's Branch

Mary Green hadn't lived in her trailer home on the outskirts of Dodson's Branch for long when she noticed something was fishy. Late at night, she'd often spy dark figures pass beneath the porch lights while her husband was away at work. Spooky. She kept a gun close and her children even closer. But she never actually saw anyone—at first.

Things got even weirder as time passed: Mary would hear eerie screaming coming from the woods in the middle of the night, and someone continued to break into her family's basement (once they built their house and relocated from the trailer) and clean all the meat out of the freezer. Her daughters were actually the first ones to see the strange hairy men in the flesh. But the Green family didn't want to be vocal about their discoveries—that they were encountering the legendary Sasquatch—for fear of being pegged "crazy." Instead, Mary wrote a book about her findings, titled *50 Years with Bigfoot: A Story of Co-Existence*.

Dodson's Branch isn't the only place where Sasquatch sightings have occurred; in fact, there are many rural areas throughout Middle and East Tennessee where Bigfoot supposedly resides. In 2004 a team of Russian researchers heard the buzz about the possible Sasquatch inhabitants and found their way to Dodson's Branch as part of a field study. They weren't disappointed. Guided by Mary, they saw twisted tree structures way up in the air, and were pelted by big rocks from the tops of the trees. The throwers of the rocks were never spotted.

Later, Mary finally did spot the Sasquatch and captured one wandering around the woods on video. Who—or what—it was exactly remains unknown.

Waste Not, Want Not

As if Tennessee did not already have enough fodder to be the butt of jokes in other states' eyes, the government had to go and further the state stereotype by passing a bill in 1999 allowing the consumption of roadkill. Yes, roadkill. If you hit it, you can eat it—raccoons, possums, deer, you name it. This screwball law actually has a bit of logical reasoning behind it, though, as many wild animals are mowed down by cars, particularly in the mountainous regions, and their carcasses left to litter the roads. The law supposedly only applies to those animals that were "accidentally" killed (though who's to judge in what unlawful manner Bambi was murdered?).

One of the more humorous exchanges came when state representative Tommy Head, who sponsored the bill in the house, offered his two cents in the *New York Times*: "There are a lot of rural people in this state who understand what this is about. Personally, I don't care for coon. I don't like the taste of coon. But we've got a lot of people at home who have coon dogs and hunt for coon. Of course, not with their cars." He later went on to say, "If you've messed up your car hitting a deer, at least you ought to be able to take it home and eat it." It should further be noted that the speaker of the Tennessee house at the time, Jimmy Naifeh, is known to sponsor a coon supper annually. Only in Tennessee, folks, only in Tennessee.

Amish Country

Ethridge

Horse-drawn carriages clop down the streets. Men chop firewood, while women churn butter. Farmers haul loads of sugarcane to molasses farms along the side of the road. Haystacks form rows of tepees in the fields that seem to never end. It's a ways from Pennsylvania—800 or so miles—but that doesn't stop Ethridge from boasting its own small Amish Country.

Tennessee's Amish enclave has been in existence in Lawrence County since 1944; today around 300 Amish farms occupy the region. And, understandably, it's started to cater to tourists as well (though it is, for the most part, authentic). You'll find Amish Country Galleries, where locally made furniture, dolls, quilts, and other crafts are featured; the owner, who surprisingly is not Amish, can give you an earful of the region's history and the Amish ways if you ask nicely. The town's homes also beckon visitors with signs for the fruits of their labors—from pickles to peanuts—signaling what each house has to offer.

All of the townsfolk are appropriately dressed, too: the men in blue shirts, black trousers, and straw hats; the women decked out in ankle-length dresses and black aprons. They even speak a different language than the rest of Tennessee (the two native languages of which are English and hillbilly, of course), a form of German that is taught to them as children.

The Old West–style Amish Country Mall & Cafe has even more memorabilia as well as the best darn fried bologna sandwich around (and pie, lots and lots of melt-in-your-mouth pie). If you'd rather someone guide you around town, you can hop aboard one of Jerry's Amish Wagon Tours, which explore the sights of Ethridge from covered wagon.

Ethridge is located about 30 miles southwest of Columbia off TN 6. For more information, call (931) 829-5055 or visit www.jerrysamish wagontours.com.

★ ★

A Little Bit Country, a Little Bit Rock 'n' Roll
Franklin

This bustling, hoity-toity burb of Nashville to the southwest is no longer home to just country music good ol' boys like George Strait, Tim McGraw, and Vince Gill. Rather, mainstream A-listers like Jessica Simpson, Jewel, Nicole Kidman, and James Marsden have been drawn to the charming city (population 42,000 and always growing) in the heart of the Deep and Dirty South, likely for its eclectic offerings, laid-back attitude, and under-the-radar vibe.

Originally an intimate agricultural region, Franklin has emerged in recent years as a high-end commercial and residential community— not to mention a ritzy enclave known for its shopping, shopping, and more shopping. Williamson County, of which it's the county seat, consistently lands the "honor" of highest average income in the state, if that tells you anything about its residents and quality of life, though those outside of Tennessee know Franklin best for its role in the Civil War (see "The Carter House" and "Dixieland" entries that follow). Prior to its occupation, it was plantation central, but that was all but destroyed once Union troops invaded and stayed put in the area for three solid years, eventually leaving the economy in shambles.

No productive day in Franklin starts without a hearty dose of hospitality and some deep-fried Southern goodness. For a quick pastry and coffee, drop in at Merridee's (110 Fourth Ave. South, Franklin, 615-790-3755, www.merridees.com), where the bakers rise well before the sun to fill your tummy with carbohydrate delights. If it's a full-on Saturday brunch you seek, don't neglect a visit to Dotson's (99 East Main St., Franklin, 651-794-2805)—it's a local institution. Here's your chance to see what grits are really all about, in case you've been deprived all your life.

From there, the majority of Franklin can be explored by foot; start and end your pedestrian journey along the aptly named Main Street and its intersecting arteries. (We have it on good authority that Nicole Kidman and Keith Urban frequent the Starbucks at the end of Main,

Downtown Franklin is a hodgepodge of cutesy cafes,
well-stocked antiques stores, and boutiques galore.

if you're into channeling paparazzi.) Just don't be surprised if you're easily distracted by the ubiquitous antiques merchants and curiosity shops galore—it's been known to happen from time to time. And, if you're not from these parts, don't forget Southerners move at an entirely different pace than you may be accustomed to (*mosey* and *meander* are fitting verbs to describe their movement). If your plastic doesn't get enough exercise on Main Street, hop in the car and head over to Cool Springs Galleria, one of the state's most sprawling and well-stocked shopping centers.

For more information on Franklin, log onto www.visitwilliamson.com.

★ ★

The Carter House
Franklin

Dubbed the "Gettysburg of the West," Franklin staked claim to one of the greatest bloodbaths of all time (at least, according to those in the infantry). On November 30, 1864, the Battle of Franklin resulted in nearly 10,000 casualties and saw forty-four local buildings turned into field hospitals. It took well over a century for the usually thriving county's economy to rebound to prewar levels.

The Carter House, an eponymous memorial to the Carter family and the many heroes of the famed battle, is a National Historic Landmark located smack in the middle of Franklin's heart. During the war

Now a National Historic Landmark, the Carter House was part of the 1864 Battle of Franklin that resulted in 10,000 lives lost.

the brick edifice was used as the federal command post while the Carter family took refuge in the cellar; visible evidence still lingers, including 1,000 bullet holes errantly scattered about.

The nonprofit Carter House Association offers daily tours of the house and grounds, which are owned by the State of Tennessee. Included are a video presentation about the Battle of Franklin and a visit to the museum with corresponding artifacts. The Carter House is situated at 1140 Columbia Ave. in downtown Franklin, within walking distance of all of Main Street's attractions. For more information, call (615) 791-1861 or visit www.carter-house.org.

The Days of Yore

Franklin

No doubt, Franklin likes to celebrate the fact that it's a town steeped in history. Though most events center around the Civil War, one annual fete takes it back even further in time. The much-lauded Tennessee Renaissance Festival relives sixteenth-century England with a host of events and activities. Those with a penchant for Shakespeare can take in a play such as *Romeo and Juliet,* which was on a recent fair docket. Those who like pretty, shiny things can peruse the artisans, who proudly display their gems and jewels, swords and silks. And those who like to eat—and let's be honest, who doesn't?—can sample some old-timey food and sip on some ale.

Villagers donning period wear wander around the premises. You can stop by and root on your favored knight in a heated joust, or pay a visit to Castle Gwynn, which imitates an authentic twelfth-century border castle. Pirates are on hand to muck the decks and swab the planks, and lure you in with romantic ballads from the sea. Other contests and performances abound, and, of course, no Renaissance fair is complete without a jester present.

The Tennessee Renaissance Festival generally runs every Saturday and Sunday throughout the month of May. For more information, call (615) 395-9950 or visit www.tnrenfest.com.

★ ★

Dixieland
Franklin

One of the most celebrated plantations in the state, Carnton was a crucial component during the Battle of Franklin in 1864, a monumental occasion that shaped the city's history and identity (see "The Carter House" entry for more information on the battle itself). The 1,400-acre house and farm were originally built with slave labor in 1815 by Virginia-born Randal McGavock, a local politician. In the 1820s his family moved onto the land, and after he died in 1843, his son John took over the place. The McGavock estate was both a horse-breeding farm and a lucrative producer of crops like potatoes and wheat.

During the Battle of Franklin, Carnton became a hospital of sorts, as it was a mere mile from the battlefield and was where the wounded would retreat. Some were tended to; others died at the house. After the war ended, John and his wife created a burial place for the many Confederate soldiers who had died at their home.

The house remained in the family's possession until 1911, when it was sold. In 1977 the house and ten acres were donated to the Carnton Association, and today, after much repair and renovation, it's on the National Register of Historic Places. You can visit the cemetery, gardens, original home, and more. There are even regular ghost tours that take you through what are considered to be Tennessee's most haunted places.

The Carnton Plantation is located at 1345 Carnton Lane in Franklin. For more information, call (615) 794-0903 or visit www.carnton.org.

Nearby is the site of the Assault on the Cotton Gin, another historic spot during the fateful Battle of Franklin. Confederate major general Patrick Cleburne reportedly perished in gruesome combat here at the location of the Carter family's former cotton gin alongside many other soldiers. Just a few years back, the plot was purchased by the city, and a pyramid of cannonballs was erected to remember that day in history.

The memorial is located at 1259 Columbia on the way to Carnton Plantation. For more information, call (615) 794-2103.

This pyramid of cannonballs was erected as a memorial to the Assault on the Cotton Gin during the Civil War.

Tennessee's Silent Sentinels

Some of the state's most noted residents are not celebrities—they're not country music stars, they're not politicians, they're not designers, they're not artists. They are, quite simply, trees. More than 200 champion and co-champion trees all over the state have been placed on a special list: the Tennessee Landmark and Historic Tree Register. Here are some of the region's finest, should you want to stop and pose with one of the heroes itself:

- Bristol: A shady spot during both the Revolutionary and Civil Wars—for soldiers, farmers, and slaves alike—the King Oak of Bristol matured during the Watauga era. Most of its family was removed, but it stands proud in the center of a city park.

- Jackson: Daniel Boone and his posse left their marks, in the form of their John Hancocks, on a beech tree during a hunting party.

- McMinnville: The Birthing Tree was a landmark on the route took by travelers who attempted the great migration, the Manifest Destiny, from Virginia to Kentucky. It was said to be good luck if a child was born under its strong branches.

- Nashville: With visible scars lingering from an epic Civil War battle, the Battle of Nashville Oak serves as a reminder of the struggle that took place in what is now Battle of Nashville Monument Park.

(Information obtained via a public document by Tom Simpson, regional urban forester for the Tennessee Department of Agriculture, Forestry Division.)

The Dearly Departed

Hohenwald

Long after he made a name for himself as half of the famed duo Lewis and Clark, explorer Meriwether Lewis, a Virginia native, was on his way from Saint Louis to Washington, D.C., to settle some unresolved matters. The first part of his journey was done by water, but he had a change of heart midway down the Mississippi River—the entire journey was initially meant to be made by water—and switched to an overland route instead. He traveled along the Natchez Trace—a 440-mile trail that stretches from Natchez, Mississippi, all the way to Nashville—and stopped in Grinder's Stand, an inn just east of Hohenwald along the trail, on October 10, 1809.

After downing some whiskey and having a bite to eat, Lewis retired to his room. The innkeeper's wife noted that Lewis was acting rather odd. A few hours later, near dawn, she heard gunshots. Lewis was dead. To this day, it's unknown if his death was a suicide or accident (the innkeeper's wife heard him crying for help, so it's possible someone could have slipped in and murdered him). They buried him nearby in Hohenwald, and the State of Tennessee erected a monument in his honor. In October 2009 there was a bicentennial celebration of Lewis's life; more than 2,500 people showed up to pay their respects.

Operation Dumbo Drop

Hohenwald

Like the safari park in Alamo, one doesn't exactly expect to be cruising the Natchez Trace Parkway and hear an elephant trumpet. But roughly twenty of the gargantuan mammals call the town of Hohenwald home, where a natural habitat refuge was developed just for them and aptly dubbed the Elephant Sanctuary.

Spanning 2,700 acres, the park is run by a nonprofit organization and licensed by the U.S. Department of Agriculture and Tennessee

Wildlife Resources Agency. It's a good thing the park covers so much ground, too, as elephants lumber along anywhere from 3 to 15 miles daily. All elephants at the park are female, as it's unnatural for males and females to live together in the wild. Typically, only nursing baby boys live with the matriarchs, and that's why at this time the Hohenwald sanctuary only takes in lady elephants, of both African and Asian descent.

The park's first resident was a retired circus elephant, Tarra, in 1995; since then a couple dozen pachyderms have called the sanctuary home. The place was founded by Carol Buckley and Scott Blais, who started the sanctuary as a means to create a haven for elderly elephants in a beautiful and serene setting, as well as educate the public about the many threats to the endangered animals. The duo had a longtime affinity for elephants, as both had cared for and managed them in captivity for decades, so it was only natural that they eventually started their own organization.

At press time, the sanctuary was not open to the public, though plans are in the works to create an education complex that would change that. For more information on the sanctuary, visit www .elephants.com.

King of the Wild Frontier

Lawrenceburg

Round these parts, you can't pass a park or town square that doesn't pay tribute to one of the region's finest former inhabitants. And you can't drive through Lawrenceburg, a 10,000-person rural town near the Alabama border inhabited by Hernando de Soto many centuries ago, without passing every last gas station and convenience store memorializing the hometown hero: David Crockett. While the former congressman is perhaps best remembered for his Alamo days in Texas, where he perished in battle, he was born in Limestone, Tennessee, and spent the bulk of his years in Lawrenceburg.

For a glimpse of the homage to Davy, you need not go further than the town square, where a statue of him (complete with rifle, iconic hat, and powder horn) stands tall and proud; nearby, just a block down the way on Military Street, you'll also find a replica of his log cabin office, with authentic relics protected by a glass case. In the middle of his eponymous playground, David Crockett State Park, there's also a museum dedicated to his exploits, as well as tennis courts, swimming pools, and trails and fields galore for those less interested in history.

Lawrenceburg is located 60 miles southwest of Franklin. To get there, take TN 6 south. For more information on the town, visit www.lawrenceburgtn.gov.

Antiques Central

Leiper's Fork

While Franklin has a particular (and oftentimes overwhelming) focus on all things Civil War, you'll find one other major theme permeating the area: antiques. As its name suggests, Serenite Maison features both nineteenth- and twentieth-century antiques and European mercantile, and particularly specializes in antique French linens. The shop is located at 4149 Old Hillsboro Rd. in Leiper's Fork (though it has a Franklin mailing address). For more information, call (615) 599-2071.

Just a couple doors up is Neena's Primitive Antiques, which focuses on eighteenth- and nineteenth-century antiques. Much of Neena's collections, which are known as the biggest and best Tennessee has to offer, come from an old stagecoach stop. Some of the items you might stumble upon—from doll carriages and mantles to church pews and clothing—are early settler, Native American, and African-American antiques. Neena's is located at 4158 Old Hillsboro Rd. Call (615) 790-0345 for more information.

If you haven't had enough antiques for one day, the Franklin Antique Mall at 251 Second Ave. in downtown Franklin will, no doubt, satisfy your craving. For more information, call (615) 790-8593.

★ ★

A Little Bit of Everything, All Rolled into One
Leiper's Fork

You've heard the term *one-stop shop,* but do you know who invented it? That would be Puckett's Grocery and Restaurant in Leiper's Fork, a quirky pit stop on the outskirts of Franklin. (OK, not really, but they might as well have.) A full-fledged, down-home, Southern-style restaurant paired with a gas station, paired with a grocery store, paired with a live music venue: Does it get any more all-consuming—not to mention better—than that?

The eponymous stop, which was founded by the Puckett family in the 1950s, has since opened two additional locations in Franklin and Nashville; it's famous for its "real food, real people and real atmosphere" slogan. (In fact, it's so "real," all the tables and chairs and other furniture are mismatched.) You'll see motorcyclists, you'll see locals, you'll see road trippers, you'll see hikers fresh off the Natchez Trace, you'll see farmers straight off of the fields. Heck, you might even spot a celebrity or two, as many call Williamson County home.

Regulars swear by the BBQ sandwich and chocolate chess pie as the recipe for a perfect afternoon. Most weekend nights, particularly during the sweaty summers, you'll catch many a local band (and sometimes big names like Brad Paisley or the Judds if luck is on your side) taking the stage in the Lawnchair Theater.

Puckett's is located at 4142 Old Hillsboro Rd. in Leiper's Fork, about 10 miles southwest of downtown Franklin. For more information, call (615) 794-1308 or visit www.puckettsgrocery.com.

Ye Olde Bookstore
Leiper's Fork

In continuing the "old and used" mentality of Leiper's Fork, Yeoman's in the Fork is lauded as not just the best rare bookstore in the state, but in the entire Southeast as well. In fact, its tagline is "the small town bookshop with uptown books."

The owners spent more than a decade curating their collections and understanding the history of it all before opening the shop in 2009 and recruiting fellow enthusiasts, colleagues, and friends to come work for them. But it isn't their passion and knowledge and the diverse selection alone that deem this shop worthy of a gander. The artistry—handcrafted cherry shelves, cabinets, and display cases, along with other design touches—makes the interior quite the stunner, and the establishment itself is in one of the town's most historic homes, having been built in 1881.

The near-mint-condition volumes with their ancient covers are both well loved and well preserved. The treasure trove of books includes signed editions of classics by some of America's most beloved novelists, such as John Steinbeck and Ernest Hemingway, and encompasses every genre from medical and religion to children's reads and rare maps. There are also signed plaques by every president up to George W. Bush, as well as a bronze bench with a statue of Benjamin Franklin out front, a nod to the fact that nearby Franklin was named after the beloved historical figure.

Yeoman's in the Fork is located in Square Pillars at 4216 Old Hillsboro Rd. on the outskirts of Franklin at Leiper's Fork. For more information, call (615) 983-6460 or visit www.yeomansinthefork.com. An additional wealth of knowledge about the store and its entities is available on the shop blog, www.yeomansinthefork.com/blog, which is updated frequently by the two owners (and lifelong buds), Mike Cotter and Keith Wallace.

Gentleman Jack

Lynchburg

In Tennessee, Jack is a man who simply goes by one name, much like Madonna or Prince. He requires no surname, nor introduction. He is a man, a myth, a legend, and perhaps the state's most famous product. No matter where you are in the world, there's a distinct possibility that you might spot one of his familiar black posters etched in white decorating a bar wall, or people wearing shirts with the same insignia. He is, of course, more widely known as Jack Daniel (no *s*), the man who brought us the world's finest whiskey.

Jack was born Jasper Newton Daniel, one of thirteen children, right smack in the middle of the nineteenth century. No one knows his exact birthday thanks to a fire that claimed all court records; thus, every September, all month long, Lynchburg and other cities, states, and countries around the world celebrate his existence. Jack was given a still by a Lutheran preacher in 1866, and in 1875 he founded Jack Daniels, becoming one of the youngest, if not *the* youngest, master licensed distillers in history.

What makes Jack Daniels the brand so different is the method of charcoal mellowing the whiskey drop by drop—not to mention its look and feel. It's also made from springwater that's extracted from right beside the distillery. In the early days, Jack bottled his whiskey in earthenware jugs, but it soon became trendy to use glass bottles, so he conformed to what was popular. He opted for a square bottle, a nod to his being "a square shooter," and more than a century later, the same model is used.

Jack died in 1911 after he arrived at work extra early one morning and kicked a safe out of frustration because he couldn't pry it open. This impatient act led to his breaking his toe and developing an infection, an infection that eventually led to blood poisoning and his demise. Lynchburg natives like to tell you that Jack's experience taught them that you should never go to work early.

A visit to the distillery is both informative, encompassing both the history behind the strong stuff and the man who was Jack himself, as well as entertaining (the tour guides are known for their wit and jokes). While you can't exactly taste the whiskey thanks to that dry county law, your guide will likely lift up the top of the hops barrel and waft the fumes your way. (In many cases, that's all it takes to get a good buzz going.) You'll also be ushered through the barrelhouse,

The original distillery of the godfather of whiskey, Jasper "Jack" Newton Daniel, still reigns supreme in the tiny Middle Tennessee town of Lynchburg.

★ ★

which holds more than 20,000 barrels, each containing about fifty gallons of whiskey.

Tours of the distillery are free and offered every fifteen minutes daily. The distillery is located at 182 Lynchburg Hwy. in Lynchburg, about 75 miles southeast of Nashville. For more information on the Jack Daniel's Distillery, call (615) 883-5555 or visit www.jackdaniels.com.

Boozin' Prohibited

Despite its housing one of the world's most popular distilleries, you won't find a sip of whiskey to take the edge off anywhere in Lynchburg—or all of Moore County for that matter. The strongest beverage you'll find is tea, coffee, or lemonade.

Even after the repeal of Prohibition in 1933, the residents of Moore County voted to continue banning alcohol. And while they could reverse that decision if they really wanted, it's apparent the locals don't really see a need. Instead, you'll have to head to the next town over, Tullahoma, for all your boozin' needs. One law does allow the Jack Daniel's Distillery to sell small commemorative bottles of whiskey to tourists (enough for a shot but little else) every day except Sunday.

A Taste of Southern Charm at Its Finest
Lynchburg

Back in the good ol' days, before dinner consisted of a race to see who could shove his meal down his throat the fastest, all the while texting furiously on a BlackBerry in one hand and checking his e-mail on a laptop with the other, people actually used to enjoy a leisurely family-style meal together, with the company being the entertainment. Luckily, places like this still exist. But they don't ooze ambiance, fine food, and manners in quite the same way as Miss Mary Bobo's Boarding House does.

Owned by descendants of Jack Daniel, Miss Mary Bobo's Boarding House serves up good ol' Southern cooking in a family-style setting, complete with a local docent helming each table.

★ ★

Built in 1866 and listed on the National Register of Historic Places, the home was initially a traveler's hotel and still maintains a tradition set by Miss Mary, who ran the place until her death in 1983 just shy of her 102nd birthday: When the dinner bell rings, it's time to eat, no questions asked. Jack Daniel used to take his noonday meal here, and after Miss Mary passed, the Jack Daniel's Distillery bought the establishment. It's now owned and operated by Lynne Tolley, great-grandniece of Gentleman Jack himself.

After the sound of the dinner bell signals the beginning of the experience, a charming female docent donning nineteenth-century garb—who is always from the area—serves as the head of your table and gives you every nugget of history she possesses throughout your hour-long meal. Guests from all over the globe dine side by side, sharing the experience with total strangers (it's part of the boardinghouse's charm). Food is generously served family-style atop a lazy Susan, with every type of Southern fare you can imagine: collard greens, fried okra, macaroni and cheese, meat loaf, sweet potatoes, baked apples, fried chicken and catfish, chess pie—and, of course, sweet tea. Be sure to take a self-guided tour of the slightly postbellum property before or after you eat; there are many interesting facets such as former slave quarters.

The boardinghouse offers two "dinner" seatings a day, Monday through Saturday, at 11:00 a.m. and 1:00 p.m. Reservations are a must, and booking as far in advance as possible (as in months prior) is recommended. Miss Mary Bobo's is situated in downtown Lynchburg right off the main square. For more information, call (931) 759-7934.

More Than Jack
Lynchburg

Old Southern public squares are a shrinking wonder, which is precisely why people come to Lynchburg for a trip to see Jack and fall in love with more than the distillery. The charming square is essentially overrun with Jack Daniel's paraphernalia—shot glasses, T-shirts, posters,

While Lynchburg's claim to fame is, no doubt, Jack Daniel,
it also has a charming town square of which to boast.

the works—but that doesn't make it any less charming. (Besides, you need to stock up on the famed JD Tipsy Cake before you leave; it's the perfect souvenir to take home with you.) There are also a couple jewelry stores, an outdoors outfitter, a Harley Davidson shop, and an old-fashioned ice-cream parlor.

You'll find places to grab a bite should you not be able to get a seat at Miss Mary Bobo's table, and also the Lynchburg Ladies Handi-crafts Shop, a cooperative that sells quilts, toys, crafts, and more by local makers. The square's pièce de résistance, though—aside from the central courthouse, built in 1885 by local residents—is Herb Fanning's Old Time Hardware and General Store, which is just as it sounds, with a heavy focus on Jack, of course.

For more information on Lynchburg, visit www.lynchburgtn.com.

Bonna-what?

Manchester

It has a weird name. It has an even weirder location (some big field in the middle of a rural area of Tennessee). But that doesn't stop Bonna-roo from being the biggest fete of them all in today's music industry, anywhere in the country and possibly even the world.

A four-day festival on a 700-acre farm in a slightly backwoods Tennessee community (I'm from the area, so I can say that with author-ity), Bonnaroo sees more than 100,000 music lovers brave the 100 miles worth of standstill interstate traffic each June to watch talent from Jimmy Buffett and Tom Petty to Kanye West and Snoop Dogg take the stage. But the fest is so much more than just music—it's also a living art installation, with vendors and booths and walking canvases galore.

Bonnaroo traditionally takes place the second or third weekend of June. For more information, visit www.bonnaroo.com.

★ ★

Musical Caves
McMinnville

Sitting in a hotbed of outdoorsy endeavors—Fall Creek Falls State Park, Savage Gulf, Rock Island State Park—Cumberland Caverns is one the most unassuming of all Middle Tennessee's natural attractions. But that perhaps might have something to do with the fact that this channel of caves, one of the country's largest, is not visible on the surface, but rather found underground.

While none of the activities are too strenuous, you have the option of several different spelunking adventures, which allow you to rappel into the caverns, crawl your way through tight channels, or even spend the night in the caves if you choose. You'll see formations like Moby Dick, resembling the famed whale, and marvel at natural formations that are further accented by dramatic lighting that's used to tell a story (such as the biblical tale of creation). The caves have clearly become rather commercialized over the years, so you'll find bathrooms and a snack bar, which steal a bit of authenticity from the experience.

Cumberland Caverns is a National Natural Landmark and also lays claim to the Underground Ballroom—600 feet long, 150 feet wide, and 140 feet high—which, oddly enough, is outfitted with a massive chandelier dating from 1920s New York City and features organ music as well.

If you're going "meh" at the mere thought of yet another spelunking excursion and venturing into some of eastern America's largest caves isn't enough to get you going, try this one on for size: You can even attend a bluegrass show while you're bumming around down there. That's right, *Bluegrass Underground* is a live radio show that records once a month 333 feet belowground and airs on WSM prior to the Grand Ole Opry's Saturday night performances. And really, where can you find better natural acoustics than in a cavernous hole deep under the earth's surface? To reach the concert hall, you take the subterranean tour just like all other guests, only you'll be left in the Volcano Chamber, a giant room carved out by limestone millions of years ago, to enjoy the musical stylings of some of the Southeast's greatest bluegrass musicians.

Cumberland Caverns is located at 1437 Cumberland Caverns Rd. in McMinnville. For more information on the caverns, call (931) 668-5382. For more about *Bluegrass Underground,* visit www.bluegrass underground.com.

Clothing Optional
Murfreesboro

Looking for the perfect family vacation? Then look no further than Rock Haven Lodge, a "family nudist park" situated on the outskirts of Murfreesboro. Sounds like a Chevy Chase movie-in-the-making to me—not to mention pretty darn liberal for such a conservative state. Nevertheless, twenty-five acres of shady woodlands provide the backdrop for this au naturel retreat; guests are invited to camp in a tent, hook up their RV, or stay in one of the guest trailers fully equipped with living areas, eat-in kitchens, full baths, and bedrooms.

The resort is further kitted out with a beach volleyball court, swimming pool, shuffleboard, darts, clubhouse, tennis court—all enjoyed in the nude, of course. It also has another oddity: a miniature raceway where you can bring your own model car and enter a summer race if you choose.

Rock Haven is the only park in Tennessee sanctioned by the American Association for Nude Recreation (yes, apparently there is such a thing). It's also known for helping set the Guinness World Record for most nudists splashing in pools across the country at once—that's more than 13,000 naked bodies.

In my opinion, this is a great couples retreat, less appealing for a full-fledged family getaway. (Who wants an image of dad practicing yoga in the buff burned into his brain for the rest of his years?) Then again, maybe you're more progressive than I am. In which case, ditch your clothes and enjoy a full moon or two.

For more information about Rock Haven, call (615) 896-3553 or visit www.rockhavenlodge.com.

Hermitage Hotel
Nashville

Not only is the Hermitage Hotel Tennessee's sole four-diamond hotel, but it also has another claim to fame (aside from boasting Nashville's best restaurant, the Capitol Grille): Its men's lounge was dubbed the best bathroom in America in 2009 by an Internet poll (tens of thousands of people voted), which was covered by the Associated Press and various other media outlets.

Among other accolades, the Hermitage Hotel boasts the "best bathroom in America."

Not only can you flush in class, but you're also invited to take a seat at one of the shoeshine stations for the full VIP experience (though you may be left to do your own shining, as the bathroom doesn't have round-the-clock attendants anymore). Out of toilet paper? Pick up the Sultan telephone and call the front desk. Ladies won't be left out either, as they're welcome to take a gander at the green-toned, 2,000-square-foot space; just be respectful and make sure the place is empty before giving an unsuspecting man a scare.

While the hotel has been around since 1910, the men's room dates to 1939, and the decor reflects this period. Still, don't let the bathroom be the sole reason you visit this opulent edifice. How about the top-notch rooms, drinks in the Oak Bar, and afternoon tea in the grand lobby for a start? If you check in for the night—and you'd be a fool not to at least once in your life, even if you're a local—request a northwest-facing room on the top floor, where nighttime views of the lit-up capitol are unmatched.

The Hermitage Hotel is located at 231 Sixth Ave. North in downtown Nashville. For more information, call (888) 888-9414 or log onto www.thehermitagehotel.com.

Let's Blow This Popsicle Stand
Nashville

When a pair of sisters who grew up in Mexico decided to move to Nashville and open a Popsicle stand, they were no doubt met with some odd glances and reactions. But who's laughing now? A decade later, Las Paletas Gourmet Popsicles has become one of the most popular stops for sweet treats in all of Nashville.

The flavors—which are recipes passed down within the family and as diverse as avocado and tamarind to more "normal" varieties like pineapple (with peppers) or chocolate (with wasabi)—change daily, meaning you never know what you're in for, but one of the house specialties is chili. Tucked away in the hip 12th Avenue South hood, the storefront is nothing special, but the overall experience is something your taste buds won't forget anytime soon.

Las Paletas can be found in the Cypress Building at 2907 12th Ave. South. For more information, call (615) 386-2101 or visit www .wheresthesign.com.

It's Not Easy Being Green

Nashville

If you ask a twenty-something Nashvillian where the cool spot to hang out is these days, he or she will probably direct you to the Gulch downtown, near the central business district. Sure, it's a mixed bag of art nooks, farmers' markets, hip bars, and tasty eateries, but that's not necessarily what makes the Gulch so noteworthy. It's also the first hood in all of the South—and only the thirteenth in the whole world—to garner the esteemed "LEED for Neighborhood Development" certification, which is no easy endeavor.

LEED is the world's premier green building certification system, developed by the U.S. Green Building Council; criteria for such recognition includes smart growth, neighborhood pattern, green building, innovation in design, and new urbanism. Even more worthy of pointing out is that this area of Nashville started as a bustling railroad corridor at the beginning of the twentieth century, then was derelict by the end of the century until a band of developers injected new life and energy in the form of swank bars and vibrant restaurants into this emerging entertainment district at the turn of the millennium.

For more information on the Gulch, visit www.nashvillegulch.com.

The Man, the Myth, the Legend

Nashville

Like Madonna, Manuel needs no introduction, nor does he require a surname. In Nashville, all you need to say is "Manuel" (*man-well*) and people will know exactly of whom you speak. If you haven't heard of him, you've no doubt seen his creations. He is the artist behind and

★ ★

purveyor of "country music couture," the style of clothing that has kept rhinestone manufacturers in business for decades running.

Born Manuel Arturo José Cuevas Martinez in Michoacán, the Mexican style staple learned to sew when he was just seven years old, thanks to being one of eleven children and having an older brother who was skilled in the trade (and went on to become a tailor). After moving to Los Angeles in the 1950s, he fell into a niche, designing ensembles for acts such as the Lone Ranger, Roy Rogers, Aerosmith, and Lynyrd Skynyrd. Some of his biggest claims to fame include creating the Beatles' suits on the *Sgt. Pepper's Lonely Hearts Club Band* album cover, the Grateful Dead's trademark skeleton branding, Elvis's gold lame attire, and Johnny Cash's suave black suits. He'll be the first to tell you he's no fashion designer, though, but rather a costumer and artist.

Twenty years ago Manuel picked up and left Hollywood, and moved his wife and life to Nashville. He now owns and operates Manuel Exclusive Clothier's, where he gets to pursue his true passion, which is outfitting country music stars in swaths of rhinestones and embroidery (think Dolly Parton in her heyday). Manuel's shop is located at 1922 Broadway. For more information, call (615) 321-5444 or visit www.manuelcouture.com.

A Wrinkle in Time
Nashville

Former Tennessee state senator and later the nation's seventh president, Andrew Jackson was always a fan of parties and welcoming guests into his home. So it makes sense that the tradition continues—even 150-something years after his death.

Comprising both a museum (which opened in 1889) and the original home whose facade is currently undergoing a massive renovation, a wander around the Hermitage grounds is like a trip back in time. There are cemeteries and battlefields, slaves' quarters and a 1,100-acre plantation. The 1804 log cabin the Jacksons occupied before moving into much fancier digs sits out back as well.

Andrew Jackson once resided in the massive Hermitage house, whose rooms remain as they were when he inhabited it.
COURTESY OF THE HERMITAGE

The mansion's interior still maintains its original wallpaper and hardwood floors in places, and much of the furniture lives on from Jackson's days. The ornate wall coverings in the lobby foyer are 175 years old, and the whole place exudes an authentic antebellum feel, right down to the volunteers who guide the tours in appropriate period garb. If you really want to trace Andrew's footsteps as carefully as possible, watch the introductory film in the Andrew Jackson Visitor Center before exploring the mansion, gardens, Andrew and wife Rachel's tomb, Alfred's Cabin, and the Field Quarter Trail.

The Hermitage is located at 4580 Rachel's Lane in East Nashville. For more information, call (615) 889-2941 or visit www.thehermitage .com.

★ ★

House of Rock
Nashville

A stark contrast to Nashville's all-consuming country music scene is Jack White's (of White Stripes fame) Third Man Records. Both a label and a shop, Third Man was founded by Jack in Detroit in 2001 and moved to Nashville in 2009. It's now not only a storefront with a hodgepodge of rock paraphernalia, but also a production house, complete with darkroom, photography studio, rehearsal space, and distribution center. The shop also recently launched a live show dubbed *Third Man Live,* where audio recordings are sold via vinyl release in the shop.

Third Man is located at 623 Seventh Ave. South. For more information, call (615) 891-4393 or visit www.thirdmanrecords.com.

While Nashville's claim to fame is country music, a number of musicians, such as Jack White, who helms Third Man Records, are injecting a dose of rock into the once twangy scene.
MILES JOHNSON

A Picture's Worth a Thousand Words

Nashville

An old-school printing factory hardly seems like a place worthy of spending an afternoon, right? Think again. Opened in 1879, Hatch Show Print on Nashville's main drag is one of the world's oldest letterpress print shops in existence. Every big name, past and present, has used Hatch's services at one point or another, including Johnny Cash and Duke Ellington. On top of still serving as a printing press, it triples as a museum and shop.

In the digital age, Hatch is often credited with single-handedly keeping a lost art form alive by continuing to create classic letterpress event signage. But the posters don't just encompass musical

While on Broadway, pay a visit to Hatch Show Print, one of the oldest letterpress shops in existence, with a history spanning more than 130 years.

performances and acts: In fact, the first Hatch handbill ever produced was an announcement for a lecture by Harriet Beecher Stowe's brother, Reverend Henry Ward Beecher, way back in 1879.

Vintage posters and signs from the past century adorn every square inch of wall space, and you can purchase copies to take home with you as souvenirs. Despite their reputation for being the best—which, indeed, they are—Hatch Show Print products are extremely well priced. You could deck out your whole apartment with goods from the shop and not even come close to breaking the bank. (The shop also sells sturdy poster tubes for those who may be traveling through Nashville and want to transport goods home.) It's one of the most authentic remaining Nashville businesses and is covertly buried among the tourist kitsch of Broadway. If you're flying in or out of Nashville International Airport, you may very well see Hatch products, as they decorate the terminal walls from time to time.

Hatch Show Print is located at 316 Broadway in downtown Nashville. For more information, call (615) 256-2805 or visit www.hatch showprint.com.

Guitar Guy

Nashville

Those in the music industry will be able to tell you who George Gruhn is without a second thought. Those unfamiliar should probably learn who he is, stat. Owner of the eponymous Gruhn Guitars, a Broadway landmark since 1970, George is the man to know in the music instrument world. Much of what he sells you wouldn't find anywhere else, as many pieces are pre–World War II. In fact, some date back as far as the nineteenth century (George started out as a vintage instrument collector).

If you can finagle a tour from the man himself, you won't be disappointed. His business occupies four floors, the bottom of which is the storefront. The fourth floor is where "the magic happens," he'll tell you, as a team of highly trained professionals fixes and spruces

George Gruhn's eponymous guitar warehouse is the one-stop shop where many a famous musician procures his or her musical instruments.

up shelves of instruments on a daily basis. There's also a small spray booth in the back, which is unique to most instrument stores.

Past and present clients, many of whom George considers close friends, include Eric Clapton, Neil Diamond, ZZ Top, Roy Acuff, Johnny Cash, Vince Gill, and Ricky Scaggs. Though he has a list of high-profile customers, income is not dependent on the A-list clientele. Many of his most valued visitors are simply music lovers and collectors, who often purchase from the second-floor specialty room, where price tags run as high as $200,000 an item. But perhaps the wackiest facet of the whole establishment is George's personal office, where the walls are lined with reptiles and avian friends, including an Indonesian blue-tongue lizard, a band of different snake breeds, and his prized African gray parrot, with whom he is enamored. (Before his professional days, George studied zoology at the University of Chicago and Duke.)

Gruhn Guitars is located at 400 Broadway in downtown Nashville. For more information, call (615) 256-2033 or visit www.gruhn.com.

O Christmas Tree
Nashville

Hermitage Hotel aside, there's another lodging grande dame in town worthy of catching your eye. The Gaylord Opryland Hotel has long been a Nashville staple, but it's really the holiday season when she gets her time to shine.

Nearly two million twinkling lights adorn both the front lawn and the hotel's sprawling interior as part of the annual "A Country Christmas" celebration. Additionally, there are towering trees, festive trinkets, a Living Nativity, fountain shows, and even a gingerbread corner where children can create their own cookie men, women, and houses. Other pastimes include a guided tour of the hotel's atrium aboard the Delta Flatboat and a horse-drawn carriage ride around the fifty-two-acre property (both for a fee). The lighting ceremony, which jumpstarts Opryland's holiday season, usually takes place mid-November, and the place is lit up until just after the new year.

Visitors be aware: While entry is free of charge, Gaylord charges an arm and a leg to park, even just for a brief glimpse at the decor. You'd be wiser to leave your car in the nearby lot of the Grand Ole Opry or Opry Mills megamall, where parking is free and just a short walk to the hotel.

The Gaylord Opryland Hotel is located at 2800 Opryland Dr. in Nashville, just off TN 155. For more information on the annual Country Christmas, call (615) 889-1000 or log onto www.gaylordhotels .com.

The Gaylord Opryland Hotel becomes a winter wonderland every November and December, as it's brought to life with nearly two million twinkling Christmas lights and a whole host of festive happenings.

War of the Wings

Nashville

Tennessee's capital has been experiencing a bit of an internal war these past few years: Which of the many chicken shacks in town boasts the hottest wings? It's hardly a competition, however, as there's one clear frontrunner.

Open since 1940, Prince's Hot Chicken Shack is so far out of the way from downtown—about 6 slow miles worth of Second Avenue traffic lights—that you'll feel like you're not in Kansas (or rather, Nashville) anymore. The menu is very basic—chicken breasts, chicken

I challenge you to a chicken duel at Prince's Hot Chicken Shack. The test? Scarfing down a whole chicken leg—ordered HOT, no cheating!— without tears streaming down your face.

legs, wings at times, baked beans, et al.—and when they say hot, they mean **HOT** (capitals, bold letters and all). I ordered my chicken medium and, within bites, my brow was beaded in sweat, my nose was running profusely, and my eyes were streaming tears.

At Prince's, when it comes to chicken, they don't kid around. Just don't head there for lunch if you've got other afternoon obligations: An hour-and-a-half wait (or more) is perfectly normal, and it doesn't even open its doors till noon. Plus, the kitchen staff (who are less than friendly on a good day) take their sweet ol' time, and everything is fried up (sloooowly) to order. Nor should you expect a seat. The establishment only houses five tables, and people clamor to claim them once it opens up, so you'll likely be eating your chicken in the car or, if you're lucky, from one of the folding chairs lining the wall.

Since it's open until 4:00 a.m., Prince's is also a popular late-night snack spot, when the line is nowhere near as long as during daylight hours. If you're a night owl, you might save your visit for such off-peak hours, unless you really just want to see the lunchtime scene, which, I admit, is an experience in itself.

Prince's is located at 123 Ewing Dr. off US 41/Dickerson Pike. For more information, call (615) 226-9442.

Crazy Cooter

Nashville

Ben Jones has worn many hats in his lifetime: actor, musician, congressman, writer. You can add proprietor of Cooter's Place, Nashville's *Dukes of Hazzard* museum, to his repertoire of work as well.

Yes, the actor who originated the role of Cooter in the popular '70s TV series knows what sells. The museum is well stocked with original cars from the show—like the iconic orange Dodge Charger, the General Lee, inside of which you can have your picture taken—as well as other *Dukes*-related memorabilia, Confederate flags galore, and other bric-a-brac. Don't get your hopes up for a Ben sighting, though; he lives with his family in North Carolina.

If you're a fan of the cult series and visiting Nashville in the summer months, be sure to check out the annual CMT DukesFest at the Tennessee State Fairgrounds and the Music City Motorplex. Other cast members often pop by to say hello.

Cooter's Place is located at 2613 McGavock Pike, across from the Opryland Hotel and just off TN 155. For more information, call (615) 872-8358 or visit www.cootersplace.com.

An Iconic Honky-Tonk Legend
Nashville

Unlike the majority of tourist traps in these parts (bear in mind: It is a tourist trap, first and foremost), locals do actually frequent Tootsie's Orchid Lounge—even if they won't readily admit it. It's the classic honky-tonk, where rednecks convene to get boozy and cut a rug, its walls plastered with 8-by-10s of every country music star ever to have graced the streets of Nashville.

A trip to Tootsie's is sort of like a nonstop costume party: It's like every visitor sees it as a chance to bust out their rhinestone-studded chaps, feather boas, and pink sequined cowboy hats. It's also dangerously close to the Ryman Auditorium and, surprisingly, hot music acts have been known to venture down to this watering hole to whet their whistle after playing a big concert (Cher and the Rolling Stones are past known patrons).

The original establishment was called Mom's until Tootsie Bess bought the place in 1960 and gave it an updated feel and a better name. She had an affinity for struggling writers and creative types— aside from a cigar box full of IOUs, she would slip a five-dollar, sometimes even ten-dollar, bill into their pockets on occasion—and took it upon herself to keep them full and tipsy (hence all the famous faces on the walls). If you're wondering where the orchid comes in, well, one look at the garish exterior will answer that question. It's kitschy (read *rundown*) and packed (mainly with tourists), so know that going into the experience and you'll have yourself a good ol' time.

Tootsie's Orchid Lounge is located at 422 Broadway in downtown Nashville. For more information, call (615) 726-0463 or visit www .tootsies.net.

Sculpting in Color

Nashville

When Herb Williams had a dream that he was splicing together crayons to create works of art, he never possibly could have imagined how that one night's sleep would alter his future. Today Herb is the only person in the world to land a wholesale deal with Crayola, as he sculpts exclusively with their products and requires the use of literally millions of them per year; a single work, for example, might take as many as hundreds of thousands of crayons.

Herb's productions have been displayed in galleries and museums around the country, as well as children's hospitals, businesses, and other establishments. The innovative artist is also a curator at the Rymer Gallery, where many of his pieces can be viewed in the flesh. An Alabama native, Herb has been in Nashville for more than a decade. He created a 150-pound, 4-by-4-foot sculpture of Barack Obama out of 50,000 crayons of twenty different colors that was on display in Washington, D.C., for the president's inauguration and purchased by a local investor for $25,000.

The Rymer Gallery is located at 233 Fifth Ave. North. To find out more, call (615) 752-6030 or visit www.therymergallery.com. For information on Herb's other works, visit www.herbwilliamsart.com.

A Day at the Races

Nashville

On the Saturday before Mother's Day in May each year, Nashville is deafened by the roar of horses whooshing by the stands, hooves pounding repeatedly against the turf. All other Nashville activity comes to a screeching halt, as residents vacate what they were doing to head to the annual Iroquois Steeplechase.

★ ★

Admission is fairly cheap and can be purchased online or at the door (I recommend getting tickets before you go to avoid lines and chaos). Like all other Southern events, tailgating is a large draw; race-goers book their spots up to a year in advance (for a fee). Bloody Marys are the drink of choice, though in race tradition you'll find tailgaters sipping on mint juleps as well, and most people bring picnic lunches to enjoy on the sunny lawn. If you have the dough to spare, consider enjoying the experience from the comfort and shade of a private box. Just don't forget to stock up on your seersucker and big sun hats as soon as spring lines hit the department stores. (Note: There's no official betting, though it's common among groups of friends.)

Fore more information on the steeplechase, call (866) 207-2391 or visit www.iroquoissteeplechase.org.

A Whole Lotta Love
Nashville

Why people crowd the entryway of this OK-but-nothing-special diner-style joint is beyond a lot of locals' understanding. But they do and, as a result, Loveless is always brimming with business. I'm not going to lie, their biscuits and accompanying homemade jams are top-notch, but then again, you'll find a number of good ol' Southern cooks frying up something similar all along the Natchez Trace Parkway (like the One Stop Cafe in Franklin). Still, breakfast at the Loveless Cafe is more or less a Tennessee rite of passage, and I run the risk of being banished from the state by failing to include it. The adjoining shop is worthy of a gander; you never know what you might dig up.

Loveless does have a long-standing history, no less. It was once the Harpeth Valley Tea Room and became known throughout the land for its fried chicken and biscuits in 1951 when the Loveless family purchased the place. Although the cafe was sold again just eight years later, the famed biscuit recipe has been passed down from owner to owner to keep up its tradition and reputation. It stopped serving as a motel in 1985 (though its official name remains Loveless Motel and

Cafe), when the fourteen rooms were converted into more dining and business space.

The Loveless Cafe is located at 8400 TN 100 near Bellevue. For more information, call (615) 646-9700 or visit www.lovelesscafe.com.

Do-Si-Do and Around You Go

Nashville

The Wildhorse Saloon sits in a prominent spot along Nashville's most touristy stretch: Second Avenue. And you'll find a lot of tourists trying to mimic the two-step and line dances that keep this place hopping. But you'll also find a lot of locals who know that, touristy or not, this is about the best place in town to throw on your dancing boots and take a spin around the room. Sure it's cheesy, but what country music establishment isn't, really?

Wildhorse hosts regular big-name talent, and it's the perfect place to see both country music legends and newcomers due to the excellent acoustics. The drinks are a bit pricey, and the saloon is definitely not known for its food, so fuel up before you go (though the menu does boast fried pickles, and who am I to deny you such a novelty?). Line-dancing newbies need not fear: There's always someone around to show you the ropes. Boasting three levels and multiple bars, you can at least find something to whet your whistle if dancing isn't your forte.

Wildhorse Saloon is located at 120 Second Ave. North in Nashville. For more information, call (615) 902-8200 or visit www.wildhorse saloon.com.

Star Search

Nashville

Just like no section on Memphis is complete without a nod to Graceland, no chapter on Nashville is complete until you talk about the Grand Ole Opry. It's not merely a performance venue—and one of the world's most famous at that—but the longest-running live radio show in existence.

★ ★

It all started in 1925 with a handful of investors winning an insurance company at an auction. Their eventual motto, "We Shield Millions," ended up being the call letters WSM when the company decided to venture into radio a quarter of a century later, beginning with a local broadcast that started with a hillbilly program and morphed into the WSM Barndance. Eventually the station evolved even further and brought in talent to perform live on the airwaves, mixing legendary names with relative newcomers. The Grand Ole Opry moved locations a few times, including the iconic Ryman Auditorium, before settling into its permanent nest. (In recent years, the Opry has paid guest visits to the Ryman periodically.)

The Opry continues to air weekly live shows and houses hot country acts like Taylor Swift, Darius Rucker, and the Zac Brown Band, as well as traveling shows like the annual Radio City Christmas Spectacular featuring the Rockettes. But that 6-foot circle of oak in the center of the stage bears the mark of all the cowboy boot–clad legends who came well before.

The Grand Ole Opry is located at 2804 Opryland Dr. in what is now the parking lot of Opry Mills. For more information, call (615) 871-6779 or visit www.opry.com.

Topsy Turvy
Nashville

If you notice an interesting red-orange twisting structure down by the riverside across the way from the Titans stadium, it's not merely an art installation but a piece of nostalgia, a reminder of all the good times had at Opryland. As part of the Opryland Hotel and Grand Ole Opry complex, Opryland USA was an amazingly fun country music–heavy theme park with lots of rides and even more live shows. It operated for twenty-five fun-filled years until General Mills bought the complex and tore down the park to make way for a junky megamall of outlet stores.

The Wabash Cannonball, named for the nineteenth-century folk song about a fictional train of the same name, was one of the park's scarier rides, traveling upside down and around and around. After the park was demolished, very little evidence remained of what natives knew as the greatest theme park ever; however, tracks from that iconic roller coaster are now memorialized alongside the river in a piece of art known as *Ghost Ballet*.

The Wabash Cannonball installment is located across from Riverfront Park. To get there, take Broadway eastbound until you reach the river.

Clash of the Titans

Nashville

For a state where football pulses through every entity's veins, Tennessee only got its first NFL team in 1997, when the Houston Oilers packed up its Texas roots and fled for the Tennessee border. (Management did not like sharing the Houston Astrodome with so many other sports teams and wanted to relocate to a place where they'd enjoy their own home turf.) For the first two years, they were the Tennessee Oilers, keeping the mascot from their days in the Lone Star State, but in the third season, the team was renamed to the much more enticing (and threatening) Titans.

While they've experienced an erratic roller-coaster ride over their decade and change in Tennessee, the Titans could not have been blessed with more loyal and enthusiastic fans. Even in years when their losses outnumber their wins, fans pack L.P. Field along the river, donning the signature navy, silver, and lighter blue (dubbed "Titans blue") team colors. The stadium, which also hosts occasional concerts and professional soccer matches, holds around 69,000 people. And fan loyalty has paid off in the past: The Titans made it to the Super Bowl in their third season (2000), though they didn't walk away with the trophy. Famous Titans past and present include Adam "Pacman" Jones, Steve McNair (who died tragically in 2009), Albert Haynesworth, and Vince Young.

For more information about the Titans and for a game schedule, visit www.titansonline.com.

A Rose without a Thorn

Remember that whole little women's lib movement back in the first quarter of the twentieth century? Of course you do. What you likely don't remember is that Tennessee was largely responsible for the biggest outcome of that time—women gaining the right to vote—when, in August 1920, it became the thirty-sixth and final state needed to ratify the nineteenth amendment, clinching a victory for women everywhere.

But this wasn't without a fight from the anti-suffrage groups, who battled in a "War of Roses" all summer long. Yellow roses were the symbol of suffrage, and many local ladies made them the fashion du jour that muggy summer; to combat the movement, anti-suffragists wore red roses on their breasts. Legislators, too, sported a rose in the color of their choice. And, like the popular reality television show *The Bachelor*, it all came down to the final rose.

During roll call, the vote was dead even, 48 to 48, but in the final vote, the baby of the group, Harry Burn, broke the tie, though he was wearing a red rose—and he suffered for it dearly, too, after being mobbed by anti-suffragists. Later, when he was quizzed on why he sported red but voted yellow, he confessed that under his red rose was a letter from his mother, who strongly urged him to make the right decision—just going to show that if ever there were a mama's boy, Harry was it.

"Beautiful Pasture"
Nashville

Comprising 30 acres of lush pasture, Belle Meade ("Beautiful Pasture") once covered as much as 5,400 in its heyday—so much land, in fact, that it was its own city (aptly named Belle Meade). It was, and still is, one of Nashville's most celebrated historic homes.

Belle Meade began as a working farm in 1807. The owner, John Harding, first simply boarded stallions at his estate, then eventually forayed into the world of Thoroughbred racing himself a decade or so later. His son, William Giles Harding, was bitten hard by the racing and breeding bug early on and took over Belle Meade when John got too old for the job. William was lucky: When the Civil War ravaged the area and most other horse farmers were forced to give up their prized livestock to the armies, the Hardings got to keep all of theirs, giving them a leg up on the other breeders in the area. After the war, William became a hot commodity in the field of racing, racking up the purses left and right and eventually becoming the first person in the state to auction off Thoroughbreds.

William's son-in-law, also an avid horseman and also named William (Hicks Jackson), helped him further build up the breeding sector of the farm. When the elder William died, son-in-law William took over the bulk of the farm's operation, giving up racing entirely and focusing on breeding. As the breeding yielded strong sales, William continued to add onto the mansion, which hosted many a politician and general. However, as is common in circles of money and prominence, William did not handle the family fortune as he should, falling further and further down the rabbit hole of debt. Eventually, as a means of survival, he had to sell the bulk of the land and, finally, the historic home, too.

Today Belle Meade Mansion is a destination of sorts with places to eat, sip wine, shop, and lounge around. There's even a free book club that meets once a month for tea and literary discussion (details on how to join are available on the Web site). You can tour the antebellum house and what's left of the grounds, as well as take a look around the city's only winery.

It should be noted that the Hardings were one of the largest slave-owning families in the city; generations of Hardings worked side by side with their help, who also tended to the breeding, training, and jockeying. Even after the war, many of the families stuck around and continued their work at Belle Meade, and you'll see remnants of this archaic way of life in the still-standing slaves' quarters.

Belle Meade Plantation is located at 5025 Harding Pike in Nashville. For more information, call (615) 356-0501 or visit www.bellemeade plantation.com.

The sprawling thirty-acre plantation Belle Meade was once a thriving Thoroughbred farm and is now one of Nashville's proudest assets.
CAROLINE ALLISON

Living Art
Nashville

Open for a decade now, the Frist Center for the Visual Arts is at the forefront of the capital's evolving art scene. It occupies Nashville's former main post office, one of downtown's architectural marvels, and boasts 24,000 square feet of gallery space, offering spots to local and

At the forefront of Nashville's art scene, the Frist Center for the Visual Arts plays host to a number of avant-garde installations and traveling exhibitions.
COURTESY OF THE FRIST

★ ★

regional artists as well as hosting traveling national and international exhibitions. The rarity of this museum is that no collection is permanent; while several run at one time, you truly never know what you're going to find when dropping by the Frist. From weathered ancient Grecian war garb to eye-popping Seussian-style installations by artists like Dale Chihuly, the Frist is a grab bag of fun, informative pieces.

The Frist's focus is on art education; thus, alongside regular camps and workshops, it has a program called ArtQuest, an interactive way for children (and their parents) to immerse themselves in art. In addition to daily self-guided and docent-led tours, there's a monthly architecture tour for those interested in learning more about the landmark building. The gift shop is well stocked with locally made blown glass, jewelry, pottery, and other such gifts.

The Frist Center for the Visual Arts is located at 919 Broadway in downtown Nashville. For more information, call (615) 244-3340 or visit www.fristcenter.org.

Hot Rods
Nashville

While car racing is surely a Tennessee tradition (albeit more popular in the eastern third of the state), it's not every day you stumble upon a museum dedicated solely to European cars and motorcycles. Open nearly a decade, the Lane Motor Museum is a nonprofit organization that was established by a pair of local car enthusiasts, husband-and-wife team Jeff and Susan Lane. The original collection of seventy vehicles was a donation; since then, Jeff has spent much of his time scouring the globe for vintage models that could use a little TLC, all of which are restored to near-original specs (meaning no parts removed, as is typical in museums) and nearly all of which still run.

The museum displays 150 cars at a time, though its collection consists of more than 330 models (all can be viewed on the Web site). Most of the museum is organized geographically; countries represented include Austria, Czechoslovakia, France, Germany, Great

★ ★

Britain, Italy, Japan, the Netherlands, Sweden, and the United States. Nearly everything you'll find in the 132,000-square-foot facility is unique to our country and not often found in this neck of the woods. Select models and parts are for sale at the museum from time to time.

The Lane Motor Museum is located at 702 Murfreesboro Pike off I-40 out near the airport. For more information, call (615) 742-7445 or visit www.lanemotormuseum.org.

Jeff Lane runs the nonprofit Lane Motor Museum, dedicated to his number one love, cars.
COURTESY OF LANE MOTOR MUSEUM

Music Mania

As the official home of country music, it's no surprise Nashville enjoys a year-round celebration of music festivals, awards shows, and more.

- Gospel Music Association Dove Awards (www.gospelmusic.org): The biggest night in Christian music recognizes some of the most popular gospel and faith-based artists each April.

- Tin Pan South (www.tinpansouth.com): The popular songwriters' fest comes to town at the beginning of April. More than 10,000 music lovers come out to a variety of venues to see their favorites play alongside newbies and unknowns.

- Country Music Marathon (www.cm-marathon.com): A half and full marathon early one Saturday morning at the end of April, the Country Music Marathon is part of the Rock 'n' Roll series, which features a different band or performer every mile and culminates with one major act putting on a concert later that night.

- Country Music Association Music Festival (www.cmafest.com): Few events in Nashville see a higher turnout than the four-day music extravaganza each June that features iconic country musicians like Alan Jackson, Trace Adkins, Keith Urban, Brad Paisley, and Tim McGraw.

- Country Music Television Awards (www.cmt.com): This video awards show held in June lets viewers vote on their favorites.

- Music City Jazz, Blues & Heritage Festival (www.nbl4u.com): A different sort of music celebration, this outdoors jazz and blues feast for the senses takes place over Labor Day weekend in Riverfront Park.

- Country Music Association Awards (www.cmaawards.com): The biggest shebang of them all, it's fitting that this forty-plus-year-old awards show is held toward the end of the year, in November, at the Ryman Auditorium.

* *

Good to the Last Drop

Nashville

Christopher Cheek, one of the city's greatest entrepreneurial legends, got his start in the grocery trade alongside his son, Leslie. A decade later, Leslie got hitched to Mabel Wood and soon became president of the family business. While Christopher and Leslie were busy building up their brand, cousin Joel Cheek was hard at work perfecting a coffee blend that he sold through a local institution, the Maxwell House hotel; Leslie and Mabel were investors in his venture.

Maxwell House coffee fared OK, I'd say: What is now General Foods went on to buy the parent company, Cheek-Neal Coffee, granting the Cheeks a sizable income ($40 million—and this was back in the '20s). With their future secure, the Cheeks were able to relax a bit, so they bought a hundred-acre plot of land upon which they built their manor. Leslie died shortly after the estate was completed in 1933; the family's youngest child, Huldah, and her husband moved into the place a decade later.

In 1959 the Nashville Museum of Art's permanent collections came to live at Cheekwood, which since 1960 has served as the city's own botanical gardens. You can explore fifty-five acres of manicured lawns, filled with grottos, pools, streams, statues, crepe myrtles, perennials, dogwoods, oaks, hickories, persimmons, pines, and many other plant, tree, and flower varieties. There's also the Carell Woodland Sculpture Trail that stretches nearly a mile and is filled with wildlife and carved curiosities. Inside the museum you'll find permanent exhibits of Worcester porcelain and American silver, American paintings and sculptures through the centuries, and a collection of contemporary paintings from the likes of Andy Warhol, Sophie Ryder, Robert Ryman, and Larry Rivers.

Cheekwood is located at 1200 Forrest Park Dr. in Nashville's Belle Meade neighborhood. For more information, call (615) 356-8000 or visit www.cheekwood.org.

Songbirds
Nashville

Though it's nowhere near as old as its fellow dives and music joints
like Tootsie's, Bluebird Cafe occupies a niche all its own: It lends
the stage to composers and songwriters. Talent like Kathy Mattea,
the first to land a record deal, just a year after the cafe opened,
and Garth Brooks became household names after kick-starting their
careers at Bluebird. The big draw is that you don't have to be "somebody" to perform here; any old Tom, Dick, and Harry can get his
song heard. It's also one of the biggest celebrity hot spots in town, as
many well-known musicians come out on a nightly basis to cheer on
the aspiring songwriters, a handful of whom occupy the center of the
room and provide each other with acoustic and vocal backups as each
performs his or her songs.

In 2008 the Bluebird went from being independently owned to
being the property of the Nashville Songwriters Association International. Despite its popularity, the place is surprisingly small and intimate, with only twenty available tables and twenty-five bench and bar
spaces; thus, reservations to each session are required. Reservations
are taken online starting five days (Friday and Saturday shows) to one
week (weeknight shows) in advance of the desired show. Sunday and
Monday shows are easier to get in on, and tickets are distributed on a
first-come, first-served basis.

The Bluebird Cafe was originally opened as a restaurant and still
serves food, mainly pub fare. It's located at 4104 Hillsboro Rd. in
Nashville's Green Hills neighborhood. For more information, call (615)
383-1461 or visit www.bluebirdcafe.com.

The Stone Age
Palmyra

Don't mistake *Wickham* for *Wiccan* like I accidentally did; when I
arrived in the town of Palmyra, I was anticipating a display of witch-
craft and pagan rituals. Hardly. Wickham Stone Park was the life's

work of E. T. Wickham, who spent his days (and afternoons and nights) molding more than forty tons of concrete into a hodgepodge of characters up until his death in 1970. Through his forty masterpieces, you'll journey through the ages alongside the stone marvels, from various scenes depicting the Virgin Mary or Jesus to oxen and covered wagons to World War II memorials.

Wickham Stone Park is located along Buck Smith Road in Palmyra 62 miles northwest of Nashville. To get there, take I-24 West from Nashville to exit 11 for TN 76 West. From there, take US 41 Bypass to TN 48 South, then take a right onto TN 149 West to reach the town. For more information, visit www.wickhamstonepark.com.

Roosters . . . They're What's for Dinner
Santa Fe

Patrons in their hunting gear rub shoulders with visitors in their Sunday best at Nett's Country Store & Deli, another down-home Southern cooking joint in the middle of nowhere. It's housed in a nearly century-old building that has always been a general store. Barbara Annette Beard Dodson is "Nett," a farm-raised gal who used to visit the store for potato chips and bottled drinks as a kid. Today she owns and operates the old place as one of the most popular eateries around.

While Nett's has all the typical Tennessee fare, there are a few things on its menu that make it noteworthy: fried catfish, frog legs, and rooster fries. You read that correctly—rooster fries. Now, before you think it's probably not as gross a concept as it sounds, hear me out. They look like chicken nuggets and are made from—wait for it—rooster testicles. I'll let that one soak in for a bit. (If you want to make these bad boys at home, you can order the parts from the local chicken-processing plant in five-pound frozen boxes.)

One of the restaurant's biggest attractions—avian gonads aside—is Catfish Night, which is held every Friday and Saturday. You might even luck out and run into the Judd clan. The musical family, Naomi in particular, visits regularly and is beloved by those running Nett's.

★ ★

And if you're a hunter or fisherman, there's another facet of the place that will appeal: A handwritten sign on a small refrigerator announces NIGHTCRAWLERS $3.99 and 100% DOE IN ESTRUS $11.99 for purchase for all your animal-attracting needs.

Nett's Country Store & Deli is located at 4356 Skelley Rd. in Santa Fe, about 7 miles outside of Leiper's Fork. For more information, call (931) 682-2315.

Angels Among Us
Sewanee

High atop Monteagle Mountain is one of the most gorgeous college campuses you ever will see: the University of the South, fondly referred to as Sewanee, as it is located in the town of the same name. The campus spans 13,000 lush acres, and all the buildings are a rich, Gothic style. It has sweeping views of the surrounding valleys and an omnipotent, towering white cross perched at the tip top of the mountain. Distinguished students—i.e., the Order of the Gownsmen, those at the very top of their class—walk around proudly in floor-length robes; it's like a Harry Potter movie come to life. Even those who don't have such merit don nice clothing as part of Sewanee's old-fashioned "Dress Tradition."

However, what's most noteworthy about this quirky university is the angels tradition. An old folk tale says that the most beautiful of angels reside within the Sewanee grounds, which are marked by gates when you both enter and exit the mountain from either side. As you're leaving the campus, you must tap the roof of your car to "capture" such an angel, who will stay with you and guard over you while off the grounds; when you return through the pearly gates, you tap the roof again, releasing your guardian to return to her friends until she's needed by others.

For more information about Sewanee, visit www.sewanee.edu.

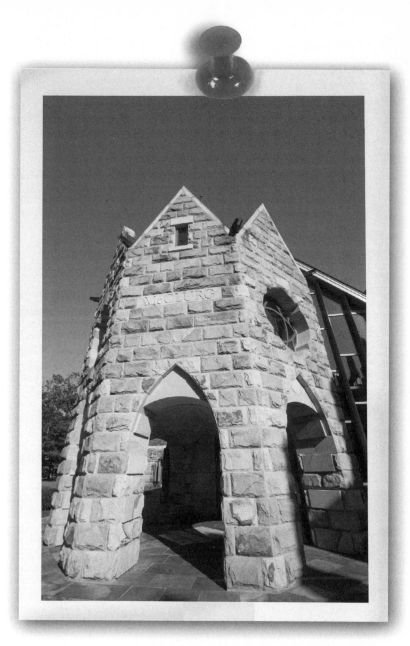

Atop Monteagle Mountain is a hidden oasis
of stunning proportions: the Gothic-style
University of the South, which is ripe with
history, tradition, and overwhelming beauty.

★ ★

A Horse Is a Horse
Shelbyville

Way back in the day, Tennessee walking horses were commonly
bred to haul people and equipment around plantations; their gentle
gait made them easy under the saddle. Since 1980 they've been the
vehicle of choice for park rangers all over the state as they patrol their
areas. They're the product of a series of breeding: A colt that was
foaled by a Hambletonian trotter and a Morgan mare is then mated
with a Tennessee pacer, producing the well-loved breed that today is
known as the Tennessee walking horse.

Their high stepping—the way they pick up their massive hooves
in an exaggerated manner as if carefully stepping over a 6-foot-high
barrier—causes many people to mistake them for Clydesdales. But no,
they're one of a kind, plus the first breed of horse to be named after
a state. And they are a reason—likely the *only* reason—people know
about tiny little Shelbyville (pronounced *shu'vel* by those who are
from there) on a global scale.

Near the end of each summer, the town is flooded by an influx
of visitors who come out for the yearly Tennessee Walking Horse
National Celebration, which runs for eleven days and ends the Saturday night before Labor Day. The tradition started in 1939 when a
horseman ventured over to Winchester to buy hay and saw a festival
going on downtown. He wondered if Shelbyville couldn't do the
same, and a lightbulb went off: Sure they could, and not only would
it be a grand fete, but one that celebrated their most famous asset
as well, the walking horses. The first festival later that year saw more
than 40,000 observers come out. Horse contests aside, there's a dog
show, barn-decorating contest, trade fair, and lots and lots of food
and booze.

The Celebration Grounds are located at 1110 Evans St. in the
center of Shelbyville, 25 miles southwest of Murfreesboro. For
more information on the festival, visit www.twhnc.com or call (931)
684-5915. There's also a Walking Horse Museum, with photos,

videos, and accolades galore, located in the public square of down-town Lynchburg. For more information on the museum, call (931) 759-5747.

What's Cookin'?
South Pittsburg

The South is known for many a fattening food, cornbread included. So it's only fitting that we'd celebrate one of our favorite fares—and annually at that—in homage to all things Southern and yummy.

The National Cornbread Festival is held each April in South Pitts-burg, a town of just 3,500 residents near the Alabama border. The initial intent of the festival was to help rebuild the town: The erosion of the tax base caused by major interstate stops all around did not bode well for South Pittsburg's future, so the locals decided to build their economy back up by promoting what they know best—cornbread.

Events encompass all the usual festival goodness, spread out over two days: There's a beauty pageant, arts and crafts, a carnival, a classic car show, a pancake breakfast, and entertainment galore. And, of course, the pièce de résistance—cornbread, of course—takes center stage in various levels of heated cooking competitions.

The festival campgrounds are located in South Pittsburg off exit 152 on I-24. For more information, visit www.nationalcornbread.com.

Dickel and Drop
Tullahoma

While Jack Daniel gets most of the fame round these parts, there's another popular man with a whiskey background who deserves his share of recognition. Those in the know will likely tell you George Dickel is even better than Jack (both men made their foray into the liquor world around the same time, near the second half of the nineteenth century), and they have a reason for claiming so: George figured out that chilling the whisky (spelled without the e to maintain

Scottish tradition) before sending it to the vats to mellow results in a much smoother product. The limestone water that comes from the nearby Cascade Springs is another contributing factor to just why George Dickel is so mighty fine.

The city's other big enterprise is Sun-Drop, a citrusy drink with a whole lot of zing (comparable to Mountain Dew or Mellow Yellow) housed in a twelve-ounce can. When mixed with Dickel, it's either a potent or a delicious concoction—depending on how you look at it. Locals claim one drink and you're hooked.

George Dickel Distillery is located at 1950 Cascade Hollow Rd. on the outskirts of Tullahoma. For more information, call (931) 857-3124 or visit www.dickel.com.

A Feast for the Senses
Woodbury

The town of Woodbury isn't anything to write home about. Yet oddly enough, it's well-rounded Arts Center of Cannon County is. Despite the rural location, the center houses an amazing art gallery, a community theater that presents such Broadway hits as *Seussical the Musical,* an ongoing concert series, its own record label, and a meat-and-three restaurant. I suppose the arts angle isn't totally out of left field, as Cannon County is rather famous for handcrafted chairs and white oak basketry. Many makers in the area extend back a dozen generations or so.

The art center is located at 1424 John Bragg Hwy. in Woodbury. For more information, call (800) 235-9073 or visit www.artscenterofcc.com.

Kapow!

It doesn't have to be the month of July for you to be able to purchase fireworks in Tennessee. While illegal in several neighboring states, Tennessee wears its affinity for explosives proudly on its sleeve: A journey up or down I-24 will have you pass by a surfeit of year-round fireworks megastores, the biggest concentration of which is located in the truck stop town of South Pittsburg and surrounding areas of Jasper and Kimball.

Growing up in such a place, I never thought anything about it until I had roommates from the Northeast, whose eyes grew wide the first time we pulled over on exit 152 and were greeted by brightly lit red and blue signs announcing the stores' contents. Even if it's barely spring, you'd be wise to stock up before the summer crowds find their way here. If nothing else, it's quite the spectacle, the type you apparently only find in these far reaches of the South.

One sight you'll get accustomed to seeing while navigating the interstates of Tennessee is firework megastores at every other exit.

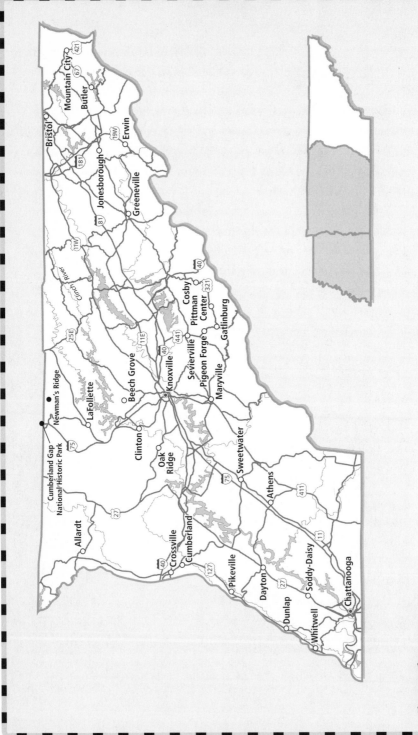

East Tennessee

3

East

The third, and *perhaps most diverse, grand division of the state is East Tennessee, which grazes five other states—Georgia, Kentucky, Virginia, West Virginia, and North Carolina—and likewise borrows a little bit of culture and tradition from all of its neighbors. While it is home to a handful of "big" cities, its most famous entity is, without a doubt, Great Smoky Mountains National Park.*

While Nashville claims to be the "home of country music," East Tennessee was actually the birthplace, thanks to the 1927 Victor recording sessions in Bristol, marking the debuts of musicians such as the Carter Family. Many a country music star, like Dolly Parton, who runs an eponymous theme park in the area, and Kenny Chesney, who continues to sing loud and proud about his origins (listen to "Back Where I Come From"), hails from these quarters.

True, the Smokies might be East Tennessee's main course, but Knoxville—the division's largest city and the third biggest in the state—is its most prized appetizer and a good foray into the world of mountain culture before you leave civilization behind entirely and head into the woods.

While Tennessee is indeed a landlocked state, you'll quickly forget this when you arrive in the region. Seven lakes surround Knox County: Cherokee, Douglas, Fort Loudon, Melton Hill, Norris, Watts Bar, and Tellico. Here you will also find the headwaters of the Tennessee River, the start of the 650-mile-long River Navigational Channel. Appropriately, the Tennessee Valley Authority—purveyor of dams across the South and the entity that brought "electricity for all" during the Great Depression—is headquartered here.

A subrange of the Appalachian Mountains and East Tennessee's crowning glory, the Great Smokies are often cloaked in a cloud of blue haze.

The Great Pumpkin
Allardt

For twenty years now, Allardt has been giving new meaning to the month of October in the northeastern part of Tennessee. While October is the month of Halloween and a prominent symbol of Halloween is the pumpkin, Allardt chooses to forgo the witches and ghouls and all other things that go bump in the night and skips straight to celebrating the pumpkin, all day, every day, for one weekend a year, traditionally the first one of the month.

In the forefront of the Allardt Pumpkin Festival is the big Weigh-Off, where farmers bring out their pumpkins to see whose is the biggest. In 2009 a Kentucky native set a record with a 1,266-pound monstrosity. There are also contests for the biggest watermelons and green squash (why, I'm still not sure), as well as prettiest in show (meaning evenly ribbed, deep orange color, no scabs or insect bites). Sizable cash prizes are distributed to all the winners. The other main attractions of the weekend are both girls' and boys' pageants with various age ranges and the selection of Pumpkin Festival King and Queen.

Aside from the gourd-like follies, there's also a fun run (in four categories: 10K, 5K, 3K, and 1 mile), a classic car show, an antique tractor show, a parade, a motorcycle show, fireworks, a costume contest, and multiple food and crafts vendors. On the Sunday of the festival, there's a "Pickin' in the Park" afternoon where musicians and singers are invited to bring out their instruments and play beneath the trees.

Allardt is located 36 miles north of Crossville off US 127. For more information on the Pumpkin Festival, call (931) 879-7125 or visit www.allardtpumpkinfestival.com. You can't miss the town; its welcome water tower is—you guessed it—painted in bright orange and meant to resemble a pumpkin.

★ ★

Who You Callin' a Fruitcake?
Athens

Yet another town named after an ancient European city, Athens has little draw for outsiders—except, that is, outsiders who have a sweet tooth for fruitcake. Heck, even those who don't are promised to be hooked on Sunshine Hollow Bakery, whose slogan is "fruitcakes for people who don't like fruitcakes."

Located on a stunning stretch of land, Sunshine Hollow Nursery grows, displays, and sells more than 1,700 varieties of dahlias, daylilies, roses, and other pretty little ladies among twenty acres and 4,000 feet of flower beds. The bakery has become popular with brides and other people catering events who yearn for a little somethin' different, as well as pretty much everyone else who has ever stepped foot on its turf. The pecan fruitcake, the main attraction, is made with honey butter rum batter, pecan halves, whole cherries, and pineapple pieces.

But fruitcakes aren't all you'll find here; Sunshine Hollow has a special place in its heart for pecans, so you'll find a variety of pecan-infused goodness, from milk chocolate covered to praline coated to chocolate toffee kinds. Other treats include chocolate-coated blueberries, strawberry-rhubarb preserves, peanut brittle, Vidalia onion barbecue sauce, and much, much more.

Sunshine Hollow Bakery is located at 198 CR 52, 16 miles west of downtown Athens off TN 30. For more information, call (800) 669-2005 or visit www.sunshinehollow.com. If your mouth is watering just reading this (like mine is) and you can't make it to Athens anytime soon, you can order their wares from the Web site.

Fast Cars and Freedom
Bristol

Wife beaters, trucker hats, and cutoff jean shorts—that's the local uniform in Bristol. Why, you might wonder? Well, for one thing, it's the Tennessee home for NASCAR. What some in other parts of the world might view as a bit redneck, Tennesseans embrace to the fullest. Located near the Virginia border in Bristol, a town predominantly know for its racing community, the Bristol Motor Speedway has been up and operating for the past fifty years. Its spring Sprint Cup Series race is considered one of the top ten in the industry and attracts fans from all over the country.

Bristol's track is unique for many reasons, the main one being that it's considerably shorter than most, which translates to much slower speeds and a whole lot of "swapping paint." Driver Mark Martin compares it to trying to fly a jet around a gymnasium, yet racers from all over embrace the track for this very reason; many even cite it as their favorite. And it got even tighter in 2010, when 160 feet of safer barriers were added. This makes for a lot more metal carnage, which makes for some happy racing fans. (What is it about burning rubber and a high volume of crashes that seem to please people so?) Other sorts of racing events, like the Nationwide Series and Camping World Truck Series, also take place in Bristol.

For more information, including race schedules and special events, visit www.bristolmotorspeedway.com.

The Town That Wouldn't Drown
Butler

In Tennessee there are two towns named Butler, but that's only because the original one was moved. Yes, you read that right: moved.

Johnson County's Butler (a town settled in 1768 that was known as Smith's Mill for the first century or so) was, at one time, physically buried under a neighboring lake on Roan Creek where the Watauga and Elk Rivers converged. Once the Tennessee Valley Authority (TVA) built a dam there, the whole place flooded, and the citizens of Butler were more or less forced to move the entire town, including many of the structures, to higher ground. The ironic part is that it was Butler's position on the water that made it such a desirable place to live in the first place: There was an abundance of water resources. On the flip

★ ★

side, there were also quite a few deadly floods, which is the reason the TVA erected the dam in 1940 in the first place.

The original town is referred to as "Old Butler," while the one remaining today is just plain Butler. The Butler Museum, at 123 Selma Curtis Rd., marks the end of one of the state's most gorgeous drives and gives the history of this waterlogged town. For more information, call (423) 768-3880 or visit www.thebutlermuseum.com.

You Don't Know Jack

In many parts of the South—particularly in the Appalachia corridor—you'll hear mention of Jack tales. These are rarely more than folklore or what is sometimes referred to as fairy tales, only the "Jack" of note is usually one of extreme weakness and significant character flaws. These charming tales, often riddled with morals, range from the popular "Jack and the Beanstalk" to lesser known titles like "Jack and the Fire Dragon" and "Jack and the Heifer Hide."

The majority of these tales derived from oral tradition and hail from faraway lands, such as Germany, and were brought to the United States when the country was colonized. Jack tales are also popular bedtime stories in other Southern states such as Virginia, Kentucky, and the Carolinas.

Always Coca-Cola
Chattanooga

While nearby Atlanta, two hours down the road, is known as the global headquarters of Coca-Cola, the first bottle actually was produced in 1899 in a plant on Patten Parkway in downtown Chattanooga. The syrupy concoction was the brainchild of a Georgia pharmacist who often whipped up medicinal beverages. He created Coca-Cola in a brass kettle in his backyard and began selling it mixed with soda water in his pharmacy.

Thirteen years after the doctor's epiphany, two local attorneys purchased the bottling rights to the drink for a whopping $1 from Asa Candler, who had bought the company rights seven years earlier. Asa thought the guys were crazy to even contemplate bottling the stuff, claiming the company's reputation was at stake (I wonder who's cringing in his grave now?). He eventually caved, however, and signed over ownership, though he never even bothered to collect his $1.

The original Coca-Cola building was at 17 Market St., a dilapidated old brick structure with a historical marker that reminds passersby of the company's hundred-plus years of history. The plant was later moved to 201 Broad St., then finally 4000 Amnicola Hwy, where it can still be found today.

Rock 'n' Roll
Chattanooga

If you've been traveling along the Tennessee interstate system and were intrigued by the various billboards carved into the shape of bright red barns donning the slogan SEE ROCK CITY, you're about to find out just what that is. A crazy labyrinth of twisting, turning ways carved into the side of Lookout Mountain, Rock City Gardens encompass fourteen acres of real estate that can be accessed via the 4,100-foot-long walking trail.

Fat Man's Squeeze, a favorite among children, is a particularly narrow stretch through a gorge where you literally have to turn sideways

★ ★

to continue. (Adults might find it ever so claustrophobic, but fear not, there are other ways around.) Grownups are more inclined to enjoy Lover's Leap, a lovely spot and panoramic viewing platform at the attraction's highest point where you can see seven states at once (though not scientifically proven)—Alabama, Georgia, Tennessee, Kentucky, Virginia, South Carolina, and North Carolina—along with a carved corn maze and some historic Civil War battlefields below. Don't fail to take the creaky swinging bridge across the ravine to this point (unless you're an acrophobe, that is).

You can easily explore the whole complex in an hour. During the Christmas season, the entire place is decorated with Santa, his elves,

From Lover's Leap, the highest point at Rock City, you can glimpse seven states all at once, not to mention farms and Civil War battlefields.

reindeer, and polar bears, and lit up in a dazzling display of holiday cheer. Rock City is located at 1400 Patten Rd., 6 miles from downtown Chattanooga, atop Lookout Mountain. For more information, call (800) 854-0675 or visit www.seerockcity.com.

I Hear That Train a Comin'

Chattanooga

What was once one of the city's main train terminals (the other, Union Station, is long gone) is now one of its most visited tourist attractions. At one time operated by the Southern Railway, passenger service ceased in the 1970s with the decline of the U.S. rail system, and the whole place was nearly demolished. Luckily, developers chose to save it and turn it into a thirty-acre resort complex instead. Today

One of the city's now-defunct train terminals has morphed into one of the Historic Hotels of America— keeping the train cars as suites fully intact.

the Chattanooga Choo Choo is one of the Historic Hotels of America, not to mention a famous number one song from 1941, and one of the only spots in the world where you can actually sleep in a once-functional train car—and a pretty darn comfortable one at that.

While the shops are nothing interesting (though the restaurants do have some decent Southern fare on their menus), the sleeping quarters are top-notch. The forty-eight Victorian Train Car suites are long and cozy and reflect the height of train-travel glamour at the turn of the twentieth century, with plenty of storage space via the old overhead luggage racks. The only real difference is you'll now enjoy cable TV and wireless Internet access.

Other worthwhile attractions within the theme park of sorts are the Model Railroad Museum, an endeavor that cost $1 million and over 50,000 hours of labor to build the 3,000 feet of track, 320 structures, and more; the colorful, well-coiffed gardens interspersed throughout the property, including more than 500 rose bushes; and the 1924 New Orleans Trolley, which takes you on an informational tour of the whole property. In 2009 the hotel celebrated one hundred years since it initially opened as a train station in 1909.

The Chattanooga Choo Choo is located at 1400 Market St. in downtown. For more information, call (800) 872-2529 or visit www.choochoo.com.

The Fall of Dixie
Chattanooga

In Tennessee you can hardly spit without hitting a Civil War battlefield. But Chickamauga, a 5,500-acre park right on the Tennessee-Georgia border, is even more notable than most. In 1863 it became the site of the last major Confederate victory and the most significant Union defeat. It also, sadly, will be remembered as the Civil War battle with the second-highest death toll; only Gettysburg claimed more soldiers' lives.

Both sides fought for control of Chattanooga, which was a vital rail center and the gateway to the heart of the Confederacy. In 1890

President Benjamin Harrison signed legislation officially declaring Chickamauga the nation's first military park; it's still the largest of its kind today.

You can visit Chickamauga Battlefield, out at the highest point of Lookout Mountain, by turning right off TN 148 onto East Brow Road. For more information, call (706) 866-9241.

Duck, Duck, Goose
Chattanooga

If you're visiting Chattanooga in the summer months and spot an amphibious ex-military World War II vehicle swimming across the river, don't be alarmed: You're not under siege. It's just the Chattanooga Ducks, the city's fun and educational driving tour company.

Tours are given in authentic DUKWs (later known as "ducks"), vehicles developed by the National Defense Research Committee and the Office of Scientific Research and Development and created to withstand strong winds and turbulent ocean conditions. The route covers much of downtown, even pausing to splash through the Tennessee River and visit the Command Post Museum, a memorial to East Tennessee's many brave war heroes. Your tour will travel along Chestnut Street to Ross's Landing (the point where the duck enters the water); under the Market, Walnut, and Veterans Bridges; around Maclellan Island (a nature preserve owned by the Audubon Society where wildlife is plentiful); and back to Ross's Landing.

Hour-long tours operate March through October. For more information, call (423) 746-3825 or visit www.chattanoogaducks.com.

Greased Lightnin'
Chattanooga

Every grease monkey in a 100-mile radius has likely visited the quirky International Towing & Recovery Museum on the way up to Lookout Mountain. Housing a collection of tow trucks and towing equipment that date back to the earliest days of the automobile, the museum

★ ★

The International Towing & Recovery Museum houses an
amalgamation of antique trucks and towing equipment,
as well as an impressive spread of toy-size models.

is a rainbow of brightly colored trinkets and parts, memorabilia, and
artifacts. There's also a small gift shop and a Hall of Fame honoring
those individuals who helped pave the way in the auto industry, as
well as a Wall of the Fallen commemorating the lives of those towers
who died in the line of service.

The museum's official mission is "to preserve the history of the
towing and recovery industry, to educate the children of the world,
and all of society, about said industry, and to honor those individuals who have made significant changes, and have dedicated precious
time throughout our industry." And for those who played with any
sort of model truck or car as a youngster, a quick walk-through will,

no doubt, prove nostalgic, as there are pint-size models, too.

The International Towing & Recovery Museum is located at 3315 Broad St. in Chattanooga. For more information, call (423) 267-3132 or visit www.internationaltowingmuseum.org.

Under the Sea
Chattanooga

Sure, you've been to a dozen aquariums. And sure, they're usually overpriced and overrun with obnoxious schoolchildren away from class on a field trip. But overpriced or not, children or none, the Tennessee Aquarium is well worth braving the crowds for, as it's the largest freshwater aquarium in the world.

The Tennessee Aquarium is the largest freshwater aquarium in the world and boasts some interesting exhibits unique to the region, like the Delta Swamp and Nickajack Lake.

★ ★

Comprising many levels of region-specific freshwater fish, such as the Nickajack Lake and the Delta Swamp sections, and some ocean critters, too, the two-building aquarium—one of which is the River Journey annex, the other the Ocean Journey—is a miraculous and iconic glass structure that has become the poster child for Chattanooga's waterfront area. Some of the aquarium's more popular exhibits include Penguins' Rock, Secret Reef, Butterfly Garden, Tropical Cove, and Rivers of the World. Be sure to check out the jellies, as well as the sea horse section, complete with some crazy-looking sea dragons. You'll need a solid three hours—maybe more—to get through each room and level. An added bonus: There's an impressive IMAX theater where you can watch the sea in 3-D.

The Tennessee Aquarium is located at 201 Chestnut St. in downtown Chattanooga. For more information, call (423) 265-0695 or visit www.tnaqua.org.

Whodunit?
Chattanooga

As you're ushered up the stairs and through the line into the dining room, it becomes increasingly evident what you're in for when you're asked to stop and pose for a photo beside a suit of knight's armor, and the knight comes to life and scares you just as the flash pops. This is no Broadway production; rather, it's community theater at its finest with an extra slice of cheese.

Dinner itself is usually some sort of Italian spread (e.g., spaghetti and meatballs) served buffet style. It's not the best food in town, but it's decent enough—and, best of all, unlimited. While everyone's being seated and starting to eat, the characters roam around the premises, stopping to talk to dinner guests and offering context clues as to which of them is the killer. Take note because at the end of the show, you'll be asked for your suspect and his or her motive. Once the show starts, audience participation is encouraged, as different guests are pulled onstage to dance or be incorporated into the show.

At the end, there's a big pop and bang and someone dies. At this point, you'll be challenged to figure out whodunit.

Vaudeville Cafe is located at 138 Market St., just across from the Tennessee Aquarium. Shows are nightly Thursday through Sunday, with occasional Tuesday performances. For more information, including showtimes and prices (reservations are required), call (423) 517-1839 or visit www.funnydinner.com.

A Change Will Do You Good

Clinton

When you think of key cities that played major roles in the civil rights movement, Jackson, Mississippi; Birmingham, Alabama; and Memphis, Tennessee, likely come to mind. You may not ever think of—or even know about—the tiny town of Clinton, about 20 miles northwest of Knoxville, which took center stage during this tumultuous period in time.

It was a stifling summer day in August 1956 when a dozen black students gathered at Green McAdoo to march down the hill to the formerly all-white Clinton High for their first day of class. Just six years prior, four black students had attempted to enroll in Clinton, but were rejected. A later Supreme Court decision (Brown vs. Board of Education), however, mandated that Clinton desegregate; previously, black students attended the all-black Green McAdoo School. While the twelve were not met with initial outrage on their first day, during the following year they were subjected to protestors who wanted to keep the school segregated, threats, and even a bombing (luckily, no one was hurt).

Tensions mounted despite government intervention, and the parents of the children contemplated pulling them out of Clinton for their own safety. A white minister, Reverend Paul Turner, took it upon himself to escort the students from Foley Hill to Clinton High on the day of the municipal elections later that year. He was beaten severely by a white mob. The principal shut down the school a week later, and the FBI arrested several locals who took part in the beating. It was nearly a decade before Green McAdoo and the other schools in Clinton and Anderson Counties desegregated.

A much more personal experience than Memphis's National Civil Rights Museum, a visit to the Green McAdoo Cultural Center is a touching account of a group of people with a whole lot of courage; those dozen students—the "Clinton 12," as they're known—will forever be memorialized in bronze outside the center. The museum is full of memorabilia, such as letters from the likes of Edward R. Murrow, pictorial time lines, and *Life* magazine spreads, as well as a mock classroom where a teacher discusses the South's "Jim Crow" era and the desegregation process. There's also a documentary, *The Clinton 12,* which is on sale both at the museum and on its Web site.

The center, which is listed on the National Register of Historic Places, is located at 101 School St. in Clinton on the hill above downtown. Admission is free. For more information, call (865) 463-6500 or visit www.greenmcadoo.org.

A History Lesson with Pizzazz
Clinton

Just the name Museum of Appalachia alone could easily instill an automatic sense of boredom. You might envision pioneers in their coonskin hats and buckskin clothes, hunting deer, churning butter, and trying to survive in the dead of winter on a snow-ridden homestead. Luckily, this is far from the experience the museum offers.

While the museum does integrate the pioneer and twentieth-century experiences in the Appalachian South, it does so in a lighthearted, fun manner. There are collections of everything from guns to musical instruments to the "Murder Bench," where two rednecks had a disagreement and a victim bled to death as a result. The whole estate spans sixty-five acres and contains a working pioneer farm dotted with cows and sheep, log cabins, and red barns. The Hall of Fame has some truly odd entities, such as a perpetual motion machine and former miner

Gol Cooper's glass eye (he poked out his eye with a pocketknife while trying to tie his shoe at the age of six). On special occasions, like the Fourth of July, for example, there are period-appropriate celebrations, encompassing archaic activities such as anvil-shooting, rail-spitting, basket-making, whittling, quilting, and blacksmithing.

The Museum of Appalachia was established in 1969 and today is a nonprofit foundation. It's located at 2819 Andersonville Hwy. in Clinton. For more information, call (865) 494-7680 or visit www.museum ofappalachia.org.

Mexican Meets Bluegrass
Cosby

For a state so far from the border, Tennessee has a helluva lot of Mexican food—and fine fare at that. (If you're not from these parts, you should know we have a pretty large Hispanic immigrant population, justifying our quality Mexican joints.) So Mexican food is hardly rare. What is out of the ordinary is a roadside Mexican stop with a bustling bluegrass scene, but this is exactly what you'll find at the Front Porch in Cosby, a town about 45 miles from Knoxville that backs the Great Smoky Mountains.

Aside from your Mexican specialties like flautas, burritos, tostadas, et. al, the Front Porch serves American cuisine such as burgers and fries, portabella mushrooms, breaded catfish, and grilled cheese. There's live bluegrass music every Friday and Saturday night during peak season, and folk music and open mic night on Sundays. It's a true oasis along bucolic 321, which is dotted with country stores and barbecue stands galore.

The Front Porch is located on US 321 in Cosby. To get there, head southeast on US 441, then veer off to TN 339 at Sevierville until the road dead-ends into Cosby, then head west on US 321 until you see the restaurant (it's very colorful; you can't miss it). For more information, call (423) 487-2875. Hours are seasonal (in winter the restaurant is often only open on Saturdays), so phone ahead.

★ ★

Swiss Family Robinson, Tennessee Style
Crossville

In Tennessee, God is often used as a scapegoat. Every last person wants to lay blame—or at rarer times, attribution—to some deed performed, claiming "God spoke to me and told me to do it." And this is exactly how the wacky Minister's Tree House in Crossville came to be.

Horace Burgess had a vision in 1993 and was compelled to build God's tree house. He told *USA Today,* "I was praying one day, and the Lord said, 'If you build me a tree house, I'll see you never run out of material.'" Though instead of a tree house—a 97-foot-tall, 10-floor, 80-room one at that—it looks more like a house that swallowed seven trees. The multistory chapel sports stained-glass windows and a bell tower; from the tower, you can see the field below with JESUS etched into it in flora. As everything is made out of scraps and recycled wood, it's a bit off-kilter and has an odd angular shape to it. Further elements include a cedar stump-cum-altar, a sanctuary with pews that doubles as a basketball court, a choir loft, and a VIP section, offering the best seats in the house.

Weird and also free; Horace is said to be very welcoming of those who want to take a gander at his creation. (The NO TRESPASSING sign is apparently for decorative purposes only. A contradictory sign at the tree house's base says WELCOME FRIENDS.) He's even allowed a handful of weddings to be held there. The Minister's Tree House is located on Beehive Lane, off exit 320 on I-40.

A Beautiful Day in the Neighborhood
Cumberland

Back in the day—the 1930s to be precise—what is now the Cumberland Homesteads Tower Museum was a part of FDR's New Deal housing/farming development. Few places were hit harder than the mountainous regions when the Great Depression swept the nation; Cumberland County was one such area where the majority of inhabitants were left jobless and hungry. The government took action and bought 10,000 or so acres of land to turn into a homestead. Barns were built first to house all the families, and the chunk of land eventually accommodated 250 homes, as well as a school, parks, and government buildings.

The tower has served as the homestead's museum since 1984, offering a great vantage point of the entire complex. At the base of the tower you'll find many related exhibits, such as photographs and documents from the '30s and '40s, as well as a gift shop. Tennessee has many historic sites throughout the state that deal with nineteenth-century history, particularly that of the Civil War era. Very few, if any others, reflect upon the more recent past, making the Cumberland Homesteads Tower Museum a true gem (aside from the cold, hard facts that the place as a whole is outstanding, the people are friendly, and the scenery is unreal). Hit up the museum en route to see the Minister's Tree House, which is very close by.

Since 2004 the museum has added another reason to visit: the annual fall Homesteads Apple Festival, a nod to the key role apples played in the lives of the homestead's original inhabitants, who relied on apple orchards for sustenance and income. Aside from all things apple-related—apple cider, apple pie, caramel apples, etc.—there are also arts and crafts booths, a quilt show, and musical talent by the likes of Amy Grant, who performed at the second bash.

The museum is open March through December. For more information, call (931) 456-9663 or visit www.cumberlandhomesteads.org.

Let's Go Ride a Bike

Cumberland Gap

Contrary to what you may think, Ralph McClanahan II, who owns and curates Little Congress Bicycle Museum, did not grow up in a bicycle-industry family. Rather, his parents were in the movie theater business, and McClanahan ran three theaters for much of his young adulthood, until he decided to change course and go into the law profession. Presently he's a district judge in Kentucky, but he's also a

★ ★

bicycle enthusiast, so he took that love and forayed into the world of bikes as well.

As a result, McClanahan opened a museum in 2003, just over the border in Tennessee, dedicated to his number one love. His collection includes seventeen mounted bicycles, in a variety of makes, with the oldest one dating back to 1895. His obsession has taken him all over the country in an attempt to procure some rare models.

Little Congress Bicycle Museum is located on Llewellyn Street in downtown Cumberland Gap, just off US 32, where the Tennessee, Kentucky, and Virginia borders converge. For more information, call (423) 869-9993 or visit www.bicyclemuseum.net.

Monkey Business
Dayton

You may have never heard of Dayton—no, not the one in Ohio; rather, the 9,000-person town northeast of Chattanooga—but that doesn't mean it wasn't once a household name. Does the Scopes trial ring a bell? If so, then you should know the Rhea County Courthouse in Dayton's epicenter is where it all went down.

It all started when a manager of a local coal company took it upon himself to propel Dayton into the national eye. He thought the best way to do this was to rouse trouble, and he hit the South where it really hurt and went straight for the jugular (i.e., religion). He talked a local teacher, John Scopes, into violating the Butler Act, which made it unlawful to teach creation theories other than biblical ones, by holding a class on evolution and Darwinism. Scopes egged on his students to cause a ruckus and testify against him in court.

This was all one big circus orchestrated so that the American Civil Liberties Union could publicly protest the Butler Act. They did so vehemently, rushing to Scopes's defense, and an eight-day trial commenced, which concluded in a nine-minute jury debate: Scopes was found guilty. He was let off with a $100 fine; his lawyers appealed to the supreme court of Tennessee, but they weren't granted a retrial (although the verdict was later overturned on a technicality). This monumental moment marked the defining point in the twentieth century when people started getting behind one of two "teams": biblical or scientific.

The Rhea County Courthouse, where the trial took place, is located at 175 Market St. in downtown Dayton.

That's a Whole Lot of Strawberry Shortcake
Dayton

Scopes trial aside—and on a far more serious note—the people of Dayton have one big claim to fame to brag about: It's the town with the most people eating strawberry shortcake at one time in the world. (I promise, I couldn't make this stuff up if I tried.)

It all started with a festival (like all good things in Tennessee do) that shone the spotlight on everyone's favorite berry: the strawberry. The fest began in 1947 as a one-day deal; even in its first year, the organizers served strawberry shortcake to more than 2,000 people who turned out to partake in the festivities. At present it's ten days long and fully encompasses the town each May.

At one time Dayton's county, Rhea, was the "Strawberry Capital of the World." But that's neither here nor there. The festival draws enough people—in the neighborhood of 20,000—to put them all side by side in a line, stuff them with the sweet dessert, and nab the record of "World's Longest Strawberry Shortcake." How's that for an honor? The rest of the fest is full of eating all things strawberry, taking part in the musical side of the event (the Strawberry Jam), derby car races, carnival rides, recipe contests, and sports tournaments and beauty pageants galore.

The Strawberry Festival takes place in downtown Dayton. For more information, call (423) 775-0361 or visit www.tnstrawberryfestival.com.

★ ★

A Dump of a Place
Dunlap

From the late 1800s through the early 1900s, the Chattanooga Iron and Coal Company ran an illegal dump: They placed 268 beehive brick ovens in Dunlap to convert coal into coke (as in the carbon variety used for processing iron ore, not the stuff you drink). When the place shut down in 1917, the ovens were all but forgotten—left to collect dust and sediment and stand the test of time. Well, stand they did, once more, when a handful of volunteers unearthed the neglected ovens in 2001. It was also discovered that they were built atop a Cherokee Indian encampment that had been used along the Trail of Tears way back when. Now the ovens are being operated as a museum in the seventy-seven-acre historic Dunlap Coke Ovens Park.

The Dunlap Coke Ovens Park is located on Mountain View Road at the base of Fredonia Mountain. To reach the park, head west on TN 111, about 25 miles from Soddy-Daisy. For more information, call (423) 949-3483 or visit www.cokeovens.com.

The Town That Hanged the Elephant
Erwin

Seeing as Tennessee is a long way from Africa, Southeast Asia, or other lands where native elephants roam wild, it might be puzzling why Erwin's claim to fame involves an elephant. The year was 1916, and war was raging overseas. Sparks World Famous Shows was one of several traveling circuses—albeit nowhere near as respected as many of its rivals—and the South was a big region of coverage for the show. Mary the elephant was part of Charlie Sparks's menagerie, and he billed her as "the largest living animal on Earth," claiming she was a few small, but vital, inches longer than his arch-nemesis P. T. Barnum's Jumbo.

A man by the name of Red Eldridge took a gamble and applied to work at the Sparks circus; he was hired as an elephant handler, even though he had no prior pachyderm knowledge and zero experience.

Shortly thereafter, Mary killed Eldridge while the circus was performing in Kingsport, Tennessee; no accurate account of how this happened exists, but the clumsy creature likely kicked or trampled him by accident. (Other stories say Mary killed him because she was in pain due to various infections, but I like to give the deceased elephant the benefit of the doubt.) The circus was already suffering, and Sparks knew he wouldn't be able to keep up his show schedule with a homicidal beast in his pack; she was, after all, already dubbed "Murderous Mary."

Various forms of execution seemed too cruel, and nothing happened when they tried to electrocute the elephant, so instead they hanged her from a derrick car with 5,000 or so bystanders watching. Mary was then buried in front of the railroad stop. It's a sad but true story, and Erwin will forever be branded by the unfortunate turn of events. If you drive along US 23 in these parts, you can stop by the Unicoi County Heritage Museum (219 South Main Ave., Erwin) to see a small memorial of newspaper clippings and pay your respects to the dearly departed pachyderm.

"It was Gatlinburg in mid-July . . ."
Gatlinburg

Gatlinburg might as well have coined the term *quirky*. A quick drive down Parkway, its main drag, makes this all too evident. You'll see musical dinner theaters, you'll see pancake houses, you'll see haunted houses (open year-round), you'll see art galleries, you'll see one of those old-timey photo booths where the ladies get gussied up in hoop skirts and the men don heavy mustaches and top hats and they all pose together for a period photo. You'll see Ripley's Believe It or Not! You'll see covered wagons parading down the street and maybe even a Civil War reenactment or two. You'll see tall people, short people, big people, small people. People with rattails and mullets, spiked do's and bouffants. It truly is a place where worlds collide—and it's all at the foot of the Smokies, too.

In the beginning it was a logging community, but these days

The quirky mountainside town of Gatlinburg houses many a curiosity shop, musical dinner theater, and oddball museum.

tourism is Gatlinburg's main industry. While the proximity to the mountains is definitely a big draw to the town, plenty of families choose to vacation here and not partake in any outdoors activities at all, as there's so much stuff, albeit weird stuff, to do in the community. It's no New York City, that's for sure, so don't go in expecting it to be. It's kitschy; it's, at times, hillbilly. But, if taken at face value, it can also be a whole heck of a lot of fun.

For more information on Gatlinburg, visit www.gatlinburg-tennessee .com.

★ ★

Salt 'n' Peppa
Gatlinburg

Where else will you find more than 20,000 sets of shakers all under one roof? Nowhere but Gatlinburg, and nowhere but the Salt and Pepper Shaker Museum—the only one of its kind anywhere in the world.

Cowboys, deer, cacti, chefs, maids, hot dogs, cows, light bulbs, and many other people, animals, and objects I bet you never knew came in shaker form . . . There's not a whole lot more to say about the intimate, family-run place—it is what it is—other than how the founders, Andrea and Rolf Ludden, summed it up: "One of the main purposes of the museum is to show the changes in a society that can be found represented in shakers. As you walk through the museum you can see the changes from ancient times to the 1500s, 1800s, 1920s, '40s, '60s, all the way to present time."

Shakers are organized by themes and colors, and most include short stories and summaries. In my opinion, the most interesting facet of the place is the drive that motivates such enthusiasts as the Ludden family to maintain such fanaticism.

The Salt and Pepper Shaker Museum is located in Winery Square in downtown Gatlinburg off US 321. In the winter months, visits are by appointment only. For more information, call (888) 778-1802 or visit www.thesaltandpeppershakermuseum.com.

He Flies through the Air with the Greatest of Ease
Gatlinburg

An adventure activity that's become quite the hit in places like Central America and the Caribbean where jungle abounds, ziplining has now come to Tennessee, too. For those unfamiliar, you're strapped into a harness, outfitted with a helmet, clipped onto a sturdy cable, and sent flying across the air, high above a canopy of trees, arms and legs flailing about. No prior experience or knowledge is necessary: Just listen to your guides beforehand, and you'll be golden.

★ ★

Gatlinburg's ziplines are more expansive than most, offering you a series of nine consecutive runs of varying lengths (other zipline parks usually only offer four or five). An additional feature worth noting is the twilight tours, something you won't find at a lot of other zipline companies.

Gatlinburg Ziplines is located at 905 River Rd., off the main Gatlinburg strip just past the tram to Ober Gatlinburg. For more information, call (877) 494-7386 or visit www.zipgatlinburg.com.

Christ Is Risen
Gatlinburg

Sure, you've heard the story of Christ being resurrected and coming back the third day. But did you know that he decided to settle permanently in Gatlinburg, Tennessee? Well, maybe not the real Jesus, but a striking likeness—or several—of him.

For nearly fifty years, Gatlinburg's popular Christus Gardens entertained and informed visitors about the life of Christ. Then, in 2008, the wax figure collection was sold to a Christian TV network and left the city. The place was torn down to make way for condos, but due to the economy and the outpouring of sorrow when the museum shuttered, it's now back by popular demand, just under a new name.

Christ in the Smokies Museum & Gardens is an exhibition comprising a series of life-size figures arranged in an array of scenes from the Bible (the Nativity, the Crucifixion, etc.). Sound, lighting, and other visual effects are implemented to bring the stories to life. Think Madame Tussauds Wax Museum, only with Jesus as the focus. A number of figures were procured from different museums all over the country; others were molded and designed by local artists. Visitors can stroll through the museum and gardens on a semi-self-guided tour, and all tours conclude in a greenhouse with a prayer garden.

Christ in the Smokies Museum & Gardens is located at 510 River Rd. in Gatlinburg. For more information, call (865) 436-5155 or visit www.christinthesmokies.com.

Channeling Seattle

Gatlinburg

A trip to Seattle is not complete without ascending the Space Needle, just like a visit to Gatlinburg is not fulfilling without trekking to the top of its own replica. Sure, you won't have a dazzling city skyline to "ooh" and "ahh" over; nope, you'll have to settle for misty blue mountains that go on for days instead.

One of Gatlinburg's tallest structures is a (much smaller) replica of Seattle's famed Space Needle. It even goes by the same name.
COURTESY OF GATLINBURG DEPARTMENT OF TOURISM

★ ★

Open every day of the year, the 400-foot-tall Space Needle has a glass elevator—*Charlie and the Chocolate Factory*-like—that you can ride to the tip top for a panoramic view from the observation deck. Those with a fear of heights might want to stay grounded: At the top, there's nothing keeping you from plummeting to the ground except a simple chest-high rail. Before you leave the facility, don't forget to stop at the bottom of the tower, where you'll find a 25,000-square-foot space, Arcadia, decked out with laser tag, a hurricane simulator, an old-fashioned ticket-redemption arcade, and more.

The Space Needle is located at 115 Historic Nature Trail in downtown Gatlinburg. For more information, call (865) 436-4629 or visit www.gatlinburgspaceneedle.com.

You're Getting Very Sleepy
Gatlinburg

Just one in a sea full of oddball live shows that litter downtown Gatlinburg, Jon Dee's Hypnotized Comedy Show is definitely a fan favorite. And how can you not love to watch a perfect stranger take the stage, be put in a trance, and made to do stupid things like cluck like a chicken while "under the influence"?

Even better than volunteering to be a participant yourself is volunteering the friends or family members you came with so you can sit in the audience and point and laugh at the ridiculousness (all the while filming the spectacle with your video camera). With a background in the entertainment biz, Jon knows what makes a show. He'll have you on the floor in fits of laughter before the curtain falls, though atheists beware: Jon's a former pastor and often incorporates a religious message into his routine.

The show takes place on the ground level of the Space Needle Family Fun Center at 115 Historic Nature Trail in Gatlinburg. For more information, call (877) 732-5497 or visit www.gatlinburgshow.com.

Santa Claus Is Comin' to Town

Gatlinburg

I'm not even talking about Christmas in July—I'm talking about Christmas in March. Before you barely have time to pack up your ornaments and mistletoe and get to missing the jolly old guy with the bowl full of jelly, he's back for the annual Gatlinburg Celebrate Santa Convention. (Guess someone at the Gatlinburg Visitor Center was on the Nice List.)

A relatively new gala, the Celebrate Santa Convention boasts a sea of Santas, Mrs. Clauses, elves, and reindeers, all roaming Gatlinburg's

Each March—no, not December—Gatlinburg comes alive with hundreds of poseur Santas and their posses of Mrs. Clauses, reindeers, and elves galore.
COURTESY OF GATLINBURG DEPARTMENT OF TOURISM

★ ★

strip in full costume. Participants "ho ho ho" their way through the Santa Tube Races, where a handful of tubby guys dressed in red go slipping and sliding down a snow-covered raceway in a tube; the Jingle Bell Ball; a fashion show featuring the latest in North Pole trends; and the Holly & Shamrock Parade and Santa Fashion Show, both held at the Gatlinburg Convention Center, which showcase period costumes and various Christmas customs from around the world.

The convention has two main purposes: to celebrate the patron saint on whom the fictional character was based, and to help those in the industry who portray characters during the holiday season improve their portrayal and, as a result, bring Christmas spirit to children in their own towns. Classes and workshops incorporate such topics as "Curl Up and Dye with Mrs. Claus" (makeup and character transformations); "Santa and the Deaf" (facilitating visits with hearing-impaired children); "Beyond the Beard and Red Suit: Improving Santa's Image" (polishing one's visual, verbal, and nonverbal skills); and "Whitening Without Bleach" (how to make your beard snow white without the use of a chemical aid).

For more information on the Celebrate Santa Convention, call (865) 244-5230 or visit www.celebratesanta.com.

A Tongue Scorcher
Gatlinburg

Carrying allegedly "the hottest sauce in the universe"—which has a label advising to "keep away from small children and pets"—the Pepper Palace's name says it all. This place reigns supreme in all things spicy and likely to burn your esophagus. But for the non-lover of hot, hot, hot, it carries all sorts of savory and sweet products that will appeal as well: dilled garlic, gourmet chipotle mustard, chili lime seasoning, sweet bourbon glaze, "nasal napalm," horseradish, candied jalapeños, cow jerky, habanero strawberry jelly, black bean and corn salsa, pumpkin butter, and whiskey flapjack and waffle syrup, to name just a few. You never really know what you might find filling its aisles. Best of all: You can try as you go.

The Pepper Palace has a whole host of goodies to sample. Try them all; I won't judge. There's also a humorous and whimsical XXX department for the over-eighteen crowd, where you'll find novelty items (Dr. Fart Hot Sauce with Fart Sounds Key Chain, anyone?) and sauces meant to be worn and used for . . . other things (use your imagination on this one).

Pepper Palace is located in Suite D10 of Gatlinburg's Mountain Mall at 611 Parkway. For more information, call (865) 436-5577 or visit www.pepperpalace.com.

Mirror, Mirror, on the Wall
Gatlinburg

Finally, a place where it's totally kosher for you to look at thirty-seven different versions of yourself in the mirror and not be called vain. The Amazing Mirror Maze is sort of a fun house–like experience, where you stumble and bump your way through a long series of mirrors and try to find your way to the other side. The music and dramatic lighting only aid in getting you more mixed up. Warning: You'll constantly have the sneaking suspicion that someone is following you, only to turn around and catch the culprit—you! If you find your way out too quickly—it's a crapshoot; it takes some people five minutes, others forty-five—you can go right back in at no extra charge.

Whatever you do, don't confuse this with the mirror maze in Ripley's Believe It or Not! which many say is a rip-off; this one is much more enjoyable. You can buy your ticket in a combo deal with the 3-D black light mini-golf course if you so desire and get more bang for your buck. Adventure Quest (2491 Parkway), at the other end of the road in Pigeon Forge, is home to a similar attraction. The Mirror Maze is located at 632 Parkway in Gatlinburg. For more information, call (865) 430-1837.

★ ★

Golfing Hillbilly-Style

Gatlinburg

A place like Gatlinburg is precisely the type of town you'd expect to find attractions like putt-putt around every bend—and you wouldn't be disappointed. But it's not on every corner you can ride a tram up a mountain, disembark, then start swinging your putter and whacking your ball through moonshine stills and tractor trailers.

Once you reach the top of the complex via an incline, whether you get off on the right or left side determines which of the eighteen-hole shaded courses you'll play. The courses aren't anything unique; it's the riding of the tram up and down the mountain—and the cool respite the place offers from atop the bluff on those humid Gatlinburg days—that makes it such a standout.

Hillbilly Golf is located at 340 Parkway in downtown Gatlinburg. For more information, call (865) 436-7470.

Paranormal Activity

Gatlinburg

Usually the only time you can locate a serious haunted house is during the month of October. And even then, it's often subpar and put on by a church or community theater with a scare factor of perhaps a five on a scale of one to ten. Unless you happen to be in Gatlinburg, that is.

The Mysterious Mansion is open year-round and will have you wetting your pants in fright. From the very beginning when you're made to find your own secret passageway into the haunted house, you're on your own to work your way through the house of terror, complete with dark, dank dungeons and winding staircases. While there seems to be only one man, a professional actor/menace, roaming the corridors waiting to jump out and seize hold of your terror, many of the rooms give you the spine-tingling impression that there is no way out, only further enhancing the sensation; the fear factor in the Mysterious

Mansion is more psychological than anything else. Plus, there's one freaky clown, and anyone who saw Stephen King's *It* knows that's enough to scare a person senseless.

Those with pacemakers or weak hearts should probably sit this one out. One thing to note: The outside looks deceivingly large, but it will only take you twenty minutes, thirty tops, to scream your way through the house.

The Mysterious Mansion is located at 424 River Rd. in downtown Gatlinburg just off the main strip. For more information, call (865) 436-7007.

Beat It

Gatlinburg

It's many Michael Jackson fans' dream to own just one small bit of memorabilia once loved or, heck, even once touched by the King of Pop himself. Those who are extremely lucky got a signed T-shirt or poster or, on a good day, something he threw out to the audience during one of his concerts. It would appear that Charlie Moore is much, much luckier than most.

Charlie, the owner of Hollywood Star Cars Museum in Gatlinburg, recently had the opportunity to purchase the 1985 Mercedes-Benz formerly owned by Michael Jackson. And it didn't even cost him a fortune either: He paid $104,000 for it at Julien's Auction at the Hard Rock Cafe in Times Square. The famous vehicle now sits on display at Charlie's museum alongside Dolly Parton's 1997 Cadillac D'Elegance and popular movie icons such as the Ghostbusters' Ecto-1, Eleanor from *Gone in 60 Seconds,* Herbie from *The Love Bug,* the Batmobile from *Batman Returns,* the Flintmobile from *The Flintstones* movie, and the 1969 Camaro SS convertible from *Charlie's Angels* (the movie).

Michael was the first owner of the 1985 Mercedes-Benz 500 SEL; the car is a rare model, as it was never actually intended for the American market and imported on a very limited basis. He purchased

171

★ ★

the Mercedes for use at Neverland, his sprawling 2,600-acre estate in Southern California where he lived from the 1980s to 2005, and later gifted the hot rod to his aunt for her birthday.

Hollywood Star Cars is located at 914 Parkway in downtown Gatlinburg. For more information, call (865) 430-2200.

A Troll for Your Troubles

Gatlinburg

If you're an observant kind of traveler, you'll notice suspicious-looking sentries posing under the guise of wooden trolls covertly placed throughout Gatlinburg. In keeping with East Tennessee's artisan theme, they're homemade goods from the Arensbak family, who have been constructing these grumpy little buggers for five decades now. While you'll find them in various shops and attractions around town, A Troll in the Park is where the bulk of them tend to congregate.

Ken and Neta Arensbak brought the art of troll-making, a Scandinavian tradition, to Tennessee when they immigrated to the area from postwar Denmark in 1949. Many a Scandinavian fairy tale and legend revolves around the mythical munchkins, and Ken wanted to bring these stories to life. He began piecing together replicas of these characters from his childhood with every material he could find out in the woods and around the Smokies. The intrigue his creations sparked spread quickly, and he started making more and more as demand increased. This snowball effect of popularity prompted the family to start 5 Arts Studio, where the five of them worked tirelessly to make enough trolls to go around, for gifts and to sell in shops. They later opened their own retail shop as well, aptly named A Troll in the Park.

A Troll in the Park is located at 676 Glades Rd., Suite 3, in Gatlinburg. You can also visit 5 Arts Studio, where the trolls are made, at 150 Troll Mountain Way in Cosby, about 17 miles east of Gatlinburg on US 321. For more information on A Troll in the Park, call (865) 436-0091 or visit www.atrollinthepark.com. For more on 5 Arts Studio, call (800) 951-2537 or visit www.trolls.com.

★ ★

The Spoon Snatcher

Greeneville

You don't find too many luxury hotels in these parts, let alone ones as splendid as the General Morgan Inn, which was established in 1884 as a railroad hotel. But, while pretty, it's not the mere facade or ornate interior of the hotel that's most notable, but rather one of its former waitresses, "Green Room Grace."

A waitress at the hotel's Green Room restaurant, back when it was still the Grand Central, Grace stuck around the inn long after her death—in fact, she's still there. For more than seventy-five years now, Grace has been haunting the restaurant, not harming or scaring anyone, but simply taking the spoons. Over the years, many a spoon has gone missing and several investigations have been undertaken, and the only thing anyone can deduce is that the culprit is always Grace, the supernatural spoon snatcher.

The General Morgan Inn is located at 111 North Main St. in downtown Greeneville. For more information, call (800) 223-2679 or visit www.generalmorganinn.com.

A Tall Tale

Jonesborough

There once was a town in a quiet corridor of East Tennessee, a historic old town, dating back to 1779, with lots of colonial architecture and pretty buildings. Before it became part of Tennessee, it was a North Carolinian entity. Not only was it the center of the abolitionist movement way back when, but it also tried to create its separate state, the State of Franklin, named after dear Benjamin, a few years after its establishment. It also has a deep history steeped in the tobacco industry.

Today this lovely little town is home to the International Storytelling Center, a three-acre property that both entertains and educates the public in its endeavors, and brings back a lost art, once a staple in Appalachia, that is no longer utilized in the Internet and digital era.

★ ★

Internationally known storytellers frequently stop by these parts to put on a show, but nothing tops the first full weekend of October when the National Storytelling Festival halts all other townsfolk activity.

The festival features adults-only events, like the Midnight Cabaret and Ghost Story Concerts to spook even the toughest of audiences. Showcases like Exchange Place celebrate ethnic and cultural diversity. If you're not a professional storyteller but still have a story you want to tell, you can do that as well, over at the Swappin' Ground. All shows take place under circus-like tents.

The International Storytelling Center is located at 116 West Main St. in downtown Jonesborough. For more information, call (800) 952-8392 or visit www.storytellingcenter.net.

It's Football Time in Tennessee!
Knoxville

If you're going to make a jaunt to Knoxville—at any time of the year, really—there's one thing to know: This is a town that revolves around football. True, this can be said for many a Southern town, but Knoxville takes game-day tradition to another level.

Boasting one of the three biggest football stadiums in the whole country—the honor rotates among the University of Tennessee, Penn State, and the University of Michigan on a near-daily basis—many sports fans will tell you that there's simply nothing like being in a sea of 100,000-plus UT fans on game day, all donning an almost obnoxious shade of orange, and all belting out the school song, "Rocky Top," every time their team does something good.

While some people roll into town to claim their tailgating spots as early as the Thursday before game day, the campus and its arteries are primarily flooded with orange-clad tailgaters beginning early morning the day of the game. They occupy every nook and cranny of the campus, though the most popular spots are the stadium parking lot; Circle Park, a large stretch of green lawn at the top of the hill; Fraternity Row, where there's always a party or ten; and the Strip (aka Cumberland Avenue), where most people park and set up camp behind the many restaurants and bars.

It's not uncommon for folks to hand out samples of moonshine, BBQ sandwiches, and spare bottles of beer to those passing by—this is the friendly, charitable South after all. Just be sure you don't lose track of time and forget to mosey on down to the stadium two hours before the game starts. The team parades down Peyton Manning Pass

There's no better place to get a true taste of Tennessee spirit (in the form of orange and white) than the University of Tennessee's Neyland Stadium, one of the biggest in the country.

★ ★

in a twenty-year-old tradition known as the Vol Walk from Gibbs Hall to the stadium, meeting and greeting fans as they go. Closer to kick-off time, the team comes running through the tunnel, after pausing to touch the I WILL GIVE MY ALL FOR TENNESSEE TODAY! sign, and bursts through the T that is formed by the Pride of the Southland marching band.

For more information and for a season schedule, visit www.utsports .com.

There's a Hero

Speaking of football, if you look closely around town, you'll see that many of the alleys and ways are named after the football players, past and present, who brought glory to Neyland Stadium. While Tee Martin was the last great hero to lead the Vols to national victory, there's one man who's celebrated above all the rest: Peyton Manning.

A good ol' country boy hailing from Mississippi, there's nary a more beloved adopted Tennessean than Peyton. While he never brought the Vols the gold, he'll always be remembered as the greatest football player to come through Knoxville. He's since led the Indianapolis Colts to Super Bowl victory, and his brother, former Heismann winner Eli Manning of Ole Miss glory, has done the same for the New York Giants. Peyton was coached by another local celebrity, Phil Fulmer, who was the head coach from 1992 through 2008, when he was nudged out— aka fired—following a losing season, much to the dismay of fans.

Come One, Come All

Knoxville

You may be confused as to why the University of Tennessee has a crazy bluetick hound named Smokey (both in canine and mascot form) running around the field on game day while the official university mascot is the Volunteer (similarly, Tennessee is known as the Volunteer State). Sure, the Volunteer seems like a weird collegiate symbol—other schools use more common mascots like the tiger, panther, lion, or elephant—but, as with most things, there's a story behind it.

Back during the War of 1812, Tennessee was the first to fill its quota of soldier volunteers. But it was primarily the Mexican War when the title was really reinforced: Congress asked for a contingent of 2,800 men to report to duty, and 30,000 Tennesseans showed up. Thus, it seems only natural that the state university would derive its mascot from such a noble trait.

A Spot of Tea

Knoxville

The Time Warp Tea Room is aptly named, given its Edwardian salon furniture, collection of vintage pinball machines, old-school jukeboxes, video games, and classic English motorcycles, though it is first and foremost a "modern" coffee shop.

Located in the mini-downtown area formerly referred to as Happy Holler—a cluster of bars and pool halls popular with mill workers in the 1930s—the Time Warp serves gourmet coffee, tea, hot chocolate, milk shakes, floats, and other beverages alongside treats like bagels, moon pies, tea cakes, and pastries. Here you'll also find the Knoxville classic "full house," a long-standing food tradition consisting of a chili/tamale combination. Classic movies and sporting events play on the big-screen TV. At night, local bands take the stage, and there are frequent open mic nights, too. If you don't find enough to keep you

★ ★

occupied (practically impossible), you'll be happy to know that the place also has free Wi-Fi.

Every second Saturday of the month, Knox Heritage's Preservation Network meets at the Time Warp to mingle and talk shop about subjects such as how to research your historic home; the meetings are open to everyone. There's also a Time Warp Vintage Motorcycle Club you can join, composed of "enthusiasts dedicated to the preservation of American, British, German, Italian, Russian, and Japanese

Wish That I Was on Old Rocky Top . . .

If you want to show some semblance of being a UT fan, first thing's first:

You have to learn the lingo. "Rocky Top" is the most well-known, celebrated hymn in all the land; it was penned by Felice and Boudleaux Bryant in 1967 and has since been covered by many a country artist. It's not the technical alma mater, but you'll hear it belted out and played by the band ad nauseam whenever you're in Knoxville.

While it would surely benefit you to memorize all four verses, lest you be pegged an outcast, start with the chorus, as it's the part you'll hear the most:

Rocky Top you'll always be
Home sweet home to me
Good ol' Rocky Top (woo!)
Rocky Top Tennessee, Rocky Top Tennessee

motorcycles." Meetings are casual and held every Tuesday night year-round, and the hundred-plus members generally ride their bikes to the get-togethers.

The Time Warp isn't the only oddity in Happy Holler, though: Its neighbors include a vegetarian restaurant, gay bar, tai chi center, exotic pet store, karaoke joint, and a roadside stand that sells hot dogs, ice cream, the full house, and pinto beans with cornbread.

The Time Warp Tea Room is located at 1209 North Central, about a mile from downtown Knoxville. For more information, call (865) 524-1155 or visit www.timewarpvmc.org.

Rock On
Knoxville

If you happen to be stumbling down Volunteer Boulevard and come across an oversize, brightly painted rock sporting a message, you might wonder what's with the hieroglyphics. Fear not, you've just discovered "the Rock," UT's canvas and unofficial message board, which has been painted over and over thousands of times since it was unearthed in the 1960s.

A university science professor, Bill Dunne, did an analysis of a sample of the rock and determined it's some 500 million years old and is a common local rock known as Knox dolomite. A bulldozer moved the rock in 1966 after workers discovered it near where the old Calvary Baptist Church stood. It was relocated to the area now known as Fiji Island but has since been moved again (in 2009) across the street to the other corner of the intersection of Pat Head Summitt and Volunteer Boulevard.

Students did not begin painting the Rock until the 1970s, but now the message changes almost daily. Artists sneak out in the dead of night to redecorate it with everything from profanities to proposals to club announcements to boasts of school spirit for upcoming athletic events.

★ ★

Southern Fried Goodness
Knoxville

Occupying a former Taco Bell, Chandler's Deli seems to operate under a front of false advertising. You see, it's hardly a deli per se, but rather the best soul food in all the land.

Charles Chandler was close to the point of retirement when he began plotting his next phase in life. He'd always had an affinity for curing meat, and after his daughter saw an abandoned building for sale, Charles and his wife, Gwen, decided to buy it. Initially it was meant to be a simple sandwich shop, but then Charles discovered the area lacked family restaurants and just like that, it morphed into a full-fledged, home-cooking, dine-in eatery. The paperwork had already been done, however, which is why it retained the name Chandler's Deli.

You enter the establishment and are immediately overwhelmed by the number of buffet counters serving food cafeteria-style, as well as the mouthwatering smells permeating your nostrils. The interior is nothing to write home about, but the food sure is: The place boasts superb fried chicken, fried green tomatoes, a plethora of casseroles, sweet potatoes, fried okra, mac and cheese, black-eyed peas, and a host of cakes and cobblers. It's the perfect spot for a post-church Sunday lunch—or heck, any meal, any day of the week for that matter. Just be sure to bring a friend to roll you out once you're finished.

Chandler's Deli is located at 3101 Magnolia Ave. near Chilhowee Park in North Knoxville. For more information, call (865) 595-0212 or visit www.chandlersstore.com.

Hot Tamale!
Knoxville

Greenville, Mississippi, native Clara Robinson runs Mary's Tamales, a longtime take-out restaurant famous in the area for serving Delta-style tamales. As youngsters, she and her deceased sister, Mary Manuel, used to go to the nearby town and stock up on tamales from the local vendor. Then, later on in life, they both found their separate ways to

Knoxville, where, coincidentally, their childhood tamale vendor also lived. They reconnected with the man, who remembered them from their younger years. As he aged and grew ill, he took the sisters under his wing and taught them the tricks of the trade. Together, Clara and Mary opened the tamale restaurant that's still up and running today.

When asked what exactly a Delta-style tamale is, Clara's been known to respond something to the effect of "What can you say? It's beef rolled in meat." They're different from the tamales most East Tennesseans are accustomed to, as they are long and slender and open on the ends. Aside from the regular tamale, Clara also serves the Knoxville special "full house" (tamale and chili), with vegetarian, chicken, and turkey varieties. Though she's nearing seventy, Clara doesn't show any signs of turning over ownership of her business anytime soon.

Mary's Tamales is located at 1931 East Magnolia Ave. For more information, call (865) 637-2033. Be sure to phone before you go: Clara closes during part of the summer and at other random intervals.

The King, Revisited

Knoxville

While another Sam (Phillips, of Sun Studio fame) is technically credited with launching Elvis Presley's career, his success was in good part due to a Knoxville local: Sam Morrison of Bell Sales Company. Morrison opted to blast Elvis's single "That's All Right, Mama" for all to hear over the loudspeakers in the public square, with a surprising domino effect. Hundreds of people of all ages and walks of life flocked to buy the album, one of whom was an RCA talent scout. You can imagine what happened next. The rep sent a copy to his boss in New York, and it was only a matter of months before RCA purchased the rights to the King himself from Sun Studios.

There's a Cradle of Country Music Walking Tour beginning at the East Tennessee History Center at 601 South Gay St. where you can learn more about Sam Morrison and the region's claim to musical fame. For more information, call (865) 215-8824.

Not for the Faint of Heart
Knoxville

Every town in Tennessee has a wealth of barbecue joints from which to choose. But it's not every barbecue joint where a pigburger is the specialty all day, every day. Said to originate in Knoxville, this legendary and decadent sandwich—a big slab of spicy burger, made with well-seasoned pork in lieu of ground beef, served on white bread and generously drizzled with a secret sauce with a big kick—is what keeps Dixson's hopping on Thursday, Friday, and Saturday, the only three days it opens its doors.

It's one of the only places in town where you can procure this delight these days, as the original establishment to create the dish, Brother Jack's, is long gone. Dixson's, which also specializes in ribs, barbecue chicken, baked beans, potato salad, and coleslaw, is no bigger than a trailer, so plan to take your meal to go. The joint is said to shutter its doors once it runs out of food, abiding by an old tradition, so arrive early or call before you go to reserve your pig.

Dixson's BBQ is located at 1201 Magnolia Ave. For more information, call (865) 525-9305.

The History Buff
Knoxville

Jack Neely is a well-known name in these parts. There's not a hillbilly or holler the local writer hasn't unearthed. About as nice as they come, Jack was a former truck driver, pile-driver crew supervisor, Egyptian museum guide, criminal-defense investigator, and magazine editor before he became a freelance writer and the go-to guy for all things East Tennessee.

For the past twenty years, Jack has penned the weekly "Secret History" column for the local alt weekly, *Metro Pulse,* which is available all around town and online at www.metropulse.com. He's also considered a Knoxville celebrity, and in "Where's Waldo?" fashion, many locals keep their eyes peeled for him at every joint or event in town, patting themselves on the back if they were wise enough to attend an event where Jack was also present.

For in-depth history about East Tennessee not found within these pages, pick up a copy of one of Neely's many historical-based books, such as *Knoxville: This Obscure Prismatic City* and *Market Square: A History of the Most Democratic Place on Earth,* online or in local bookstores.

Required Reading

Jack Neely, the go-to guy for all things Knoxville, advises picking up copies of the following East Tennessee must-reads—some fictional, others historical accounts—to gain a little more understanding about the enigmatic area where city culture collides with mountain livin'.

A Death in the Family, James Agee

The Orchard Keeper and Suttree, Cormac McCarthy

Bloodroot, Amy Greene

Divided Loyalties, Digby Seymour

Lincolnites and Rebels, Robert Tracy McKenzie

Knoxville, Tennessee: A Mountain City in the New South, William Bruce Wheeler

Tennessee Strings, Charles K. Wolfe

Valley So Wild, Alberta and Carson Brewer

The French Broad, Wilma Dykeman

★ ★

Knoxville's Beating Heart
Knoxville

Laden with pubs and shops, fountains and greenery, Market Square has been the center of Knoxville activity practically since it was conceived in 1854 as the site of the city's first market. Boasting the highest concentration of restaurants in East Tennessee, the pedestrian mall is full of all sorts of yummy delights like the venerable Tomato Head, one of

One of the city's prettiest parts, the oasis that is Market Square is filled with tasty eateries, trendy boutiques, laid-back pubs, and other such delights.
COURTESY OF KNOXVILLE TOURISM & SPORTS CORPORATION

the first vegetarian restaurants in town, and the Square Room, a bakery that morphs into a restaurant that turns into a nightclub each day.

Other businesses and establishments include Preservation Pub, a smoky venue with stellar live music; Yeehaw Industries, a letterpress print shop; Sapphire, a swank cocktail lounge occupying a former jewelry store; Vagabondia, a fashion boutique; and Oodles Uncorked, a pasta and wine bar.

Knoxville-born authors like James Agee and Cormac McCarthy even found the square special enough to describe in rich detail in their novels. It's home to a summer farmers' market (Wednesday and Saturday), monthly First Friday art openings, the weekly summer music fest Sundown in the City (each Thursday), and a yearly New Year's Eve art fete called First Night. One weekend in June, Market Square also is overrun by flour-y goodness, when the International Biscuit Festival comes parading into town.

For more information about Market Square and its entities, visit www.knoxvillemarketsquare.com.

Coming to You, Live
Knoxville

It's rare in this day and age for a major Americana radio act to do a live show, let alone a live show every day of the week in front of a studio audience, for free. But that's exactly what visitors to WDVX's studio at One Vision Plaza can expect out of the *Blue Plate Special* each weekday at noon. It's a jumble of folk, gospel, Celtic, swing, and more—you never really know what any one show might hold.

Once a month, the station further collaborates with AC Entertainment (of Bonnaroo fame) at the 1909 Bijou Theatre, the old vaudeville house recently praised by the *New York Times* as one of the best listening rooms in the nation. The Bijou show goes by the name *Tennessee Shines,* with plenty of bluegrass edge to spare. It sells out at least a week in advance, so plan your visit early. This is all a dose of nostalgia for the city, as the station hosted a live radio show on Gay

★ ★

Dubious Distinction

Knoxville may be located in the conservative South, but at times it likes to let its colors—the primary one being nude—show. Case in point: In 1974 Walter Cronkite dubbed Knoxville the "Streaking Capital of the World" after an estimated 5,000 people dropped their pants and went streaking down the University of Tennessee's main drag, Cumberland Avenue, wearing nothing at all. (Blame it on the moonshine.) To this day, the bar- and restaurant-ridden street is referred to fondly as "the Strip."

Street from the '20s through the '50s, when Acuff, Atkins, the Everlys, and Dolly were all starting to become household names. WDVX tries to re-create these days, and somehow it succeeds.

The WDVX headquarters are located in the Knoxville Visitor Center at Gay Street and Summit Hill Avenue. For more information, call (865) 544-1029 or visit www.wdvx.com.

A Woman with a Mission
Knoxville

No legitimate sports enthusiast hasn't heard of Pat Head Summitt. It's simply not possible to turn on ESPN or flip through a copy of *Sports Illustrated* and not be met by her name. Head coach of the University of Tennessee Lady Vols, a program that consistently makes it to the NCAA Sweet 16 year after year and has eight national championships and fifteen conference victories in its suitcase of accolades, Summitt has dominated the university basketball field since joining the Big Orange ranks in 1974.

In 2005 Summitt became the winningest basketball coach of all time—men's or women's, of any division—and to date has garnered well over 1,000 wins. And the worst part for her rivals and foes? She has many more years of coaching ahead of her. Many say that when she finally does retire, her record will be unbeatable, for all time.

Summitt has coached such Olympians and WNBA athletes as Chamique Holdsclaw, Candace Parker, Michelle Snow, Michelle Marciniak, and Tamika Catchings, along with many others. She was an Olympian herself in the 1976 Summer Olympics, as co-captain to the first-ever U.S. national women's basketball team, and helped bring home the silver.

Legendary basketball coach Pat Summitt is just one of many famed athletes who are honored in Knoxville's Women's Basketball Hall of Fame.
COURTESY OF WOMEN'S BASKETBALL HALL OF FAME

Not coincidentally, the world's only museum devoted solely to women's basketball, the aptly named Women's Basketball Hall of Fame, is located in Knoxville at 700 Hall of Fame Dr., perched above the Tennessee River and marked by a 30-foot-wide, 20,000-pound basketball paved with 96,000 pebbles. For more information on the museum, call (865) 633-9000 or visit www.wbhof.com.

Red Panda Capital of the World
Knoxville

It may be a far cry from China; nevertheless, the fifty-three-acre Knoxville Zoo is proud to be the "Red Panda Capital of the World." How does one acquire such a lofty title? By having the greatest success in the breeding and survival of baby red pandas, that's how—since 1978

(Continued on page 190)

The Knoxville Zoo boasts the most red pandas of anywhere in the Western Hemisphere, with nearly a hundred cubs born and bred in captivity here since 1978.
COURTESY OF KNOXVILLE ZOO

A Hodgepodge of Local Celebrities

Athletes, Civil War heroes, and mammals aside, here are some other local celebrities who have at one time called Knoxville home:

Tina Wesson, winner of *Survivor: Australian Outback*

Johnny Knoxville, stuntman, comedian, and actor

Dave Thomas, founder and creator of the Wendy's chain

Quentin Tarantino, actor and director

Polly Bergen, actress, singer, and first woman to serve on the board of directors of the Singer Sewing Machine Company

David Keith, actor

Jack Hanna, animal adventurer

Cormac McCarthy, novelist

Roy Acuff, singer

Beauford and Joseph Delaney, artists

Reggie White, NFL star

Milton Estes, Grand Ole Opry singer

Roy Evans, Major League Baseball player

Alex Haley, American biographer

John Tate, WBA Heavyweight Champion

Caledonia Johnson, former slave and Knoxville's first millionaire

John Cullum, actor

Everly Brothers, singing act

George Dempster, former mayor of Knoxville and inventor of the Dempster Dumpster

James Agee, Pulitzer Prize–winning author

Knoxville has celebrated nearly a hundred red panda births. The zoo has one other historical claim: In 1978 it was home to the first African elephant in the Western Hemisphere born and bred in captivity, Little Diamond.

The Knoxville Zoo is located at 3333 Woodbine Ave. For more information, call (865) 637-5331 or visit www.knoxville-zoo.org.

A Glowing Ball of Fire
Knoxville

One towering monument standing in the middle of downtown Knoxville might shock visitors upon first glance: It's 266 feet tall, twenty-six stories, and shines brightly like its namesake, the sun, reflecting blinding beams off of its 74-foot bronze sphere. The appropriately named Sunsphere was built for the 1982 World's Fair, the theme of which was "Energy Turns the World." It was created as a "monument to the sun, the source of all energy."

More than eleven million visitors came out to Knoxville that year to witness the Southeast's first World's Fair. Since the fair ended, the Sunsphere has been used as reception and office space. In 2007 it was opened to the public for the first time to commemorate the twenty-fifth anniversary of Knoxville's being put on the global map, thanks to the fair. Only five levels of the actual ball itself are utilized, with the fourth floor an observation deck offering 360-degree views of the city, but definitely drop by the Southern Graces cocktail lounge, a small but surreal Space Age experience.

For more information on the Sunsphere, visit www.knoxville.org.

The Sunsphere glows bright, its panels scattering
sunbeams in every direction, and stands tall as a
piece of oversize art in the heart of Knoxville.
COURTESY OF KNOXVILLE TOURISM & SPORTS CORPORATION

A City of Firts

While it has many grounds for bragging rights (see: the university sports program, across the board), Knoxvillians like to tell you exactly what they were the first to do. This laundry list includes:

- First English fort in the Southwest (Fort Loudon, 1756)

- First capital of a federal territory (Territory Southwest of the River Ohio, 1791)

- First territorial legislature in America (1794)

- First nonsectarian institution of higher learning (Blount College, now the University of Tennessee, chartered in 1794)

- First state created from a federal territory (1796)

- First capital of the State of Tennessee (1796–1811)

- First state readmitted to the Union after the Civil War (1866)

- First radio station in Tennessee (WNAV, now WNOX-AM, 1921)

- First government-owned electrical system (Tennessee Valley Authority, 1933)

The Wild, Wild West
Knoxville

Some thousands of miles from the western frontier, Knoxville still managed to experience its share of outlaw activity.

In 1903 one of Butch Cassidy's Wild Bunch, Kid Curry (real name

Househunters Headquarters

If you're a fan of all those home renovation and make-over-my-house type of TV programming, you might be interested to know that it all started here. Knoxville is the global head-quarters of cable's HGTV, one of the fastest-growing networks, having reached more than ninety million households in less than a decade.

Harvey Logan), shot a couple of deputies and escaped out the back window of a business on Central Avenue in today's hopping Old City district. Fear not: He was captured and thrown into the local slammer. But these outlaws have their ways: Kid escaped shortly after. Neither hide nor hair of him was ever seen again after he was spotted riding the sheriff's hijacked horse across the Gay Street Bridge.

Whet Your Whistle

Knoxville

Gastropubs may be the norm in more cosmopolitan cities up North, but they're a pretty unusual concept in this neck of the woods. Which is perhaps why the Crown & Goose, owned and operated by a home-sick Englishman, caused such a ruckus when it opened in two adjoining Victorian saloons in Old City.

With specialty beers brewed out the wazoo especially for the pub and upscale traditional English fare (think fish-and-chips, bangers and mash, shepherd's pie), local folks keep the house packed. Warm spring and summer nights are particularly popular, as there's a sprawling beer garden patio out back that accommodates the masses. While this place is no dive—its prices are a good enough indicator of that—you'll still find sporting events on the TVs that line the wall, so you can have your posh night out without having to miss the big game.

The Crown & Goose is located at 123 South Central St. in Knoxville's Old City. For more information, call (865) 524-2100 or visit www.thecrownandgoose.com.

Tennessee's first gastropub, the Crown & Goose, occupies prime real estate in Knoxville's Old City and is always packed to the brim with beer lovers.
COURTESY OF CROWN & GOOSE

No Funny Business

As if frogs croaking late into the night, roadkill, and fortune-telling mamas weren't enough, Knoxville has to add its own kooky law to the mix. According to the ordinance, it is "unlawful for any person to erect, construct or maintain an apparatus or device which would electrify or electrically charge any garbage, trash or refuse container or any object or structure or facility in close proximity to such container, such that any person coming into contact with such container, apparatus or structure or facility will receive an electric shock." Which is a fancy way of saying keep your electrically charged trash can under wraps.

Other weird local laws: Children under eighteen are not allowed to engage in any act of pinball in a commercial space during a certain time span; no one is allowed to ride or herd an animal in a street median (nor is it allowed to sell or give away any such animal anywhere outdoors around the city); and don't even think about photographing a pedestrian in a public place—it's strictly prohibited.

Nostalgia
Knoxville

While Walgreen's and CVS have all but engulfed the pharmacy-cum-convenience store genre, there's one authentic 1950s pharmacy (replete with an old-fashioned soda fountain) holding its own in Knoxville. While it's housed in a tacky strip mall, Long's Drug Store's interior maintains its vintage vibe, and you can still get the same ol' food—served by the same ol' grumpy waitresses on the same ol' old-school Styrofoam plates—for breakfast, lunch, and (early) supper.

The egg salad is one of the most popular items on Long's menu, and the chicken and tuna salads aren't bad either; the BLTs and onion rings and daily blue plate dinner special are always hot commodities, too. Oh, and given its era, you can't really leave the place without gulping down a rich milk shake—that would just be unorthodox. Surprisingly enough, Long's is packed with weekend country clubbers and the Sunday church crowd, so best to go on a weekday or off-peak meal time.

Long's Drug Store is located at 4604 Kingston Pike, where Knoxville meets Bearden. For more information, call (865) 588-9218.

Get This Party Started
Knoxville

Knoxville knows how to have fun—and not just on football game days. No matter the time of year, you'll likely find a festival or city-wide party in one of its many nooks and crannies. For example, in March you'll find Big Ears (www.bigearsfestival.com), an annual avant-garde/minimalist festival that got national press when it started a couple years back with a host of indie musical talent.

One of the biggest events is the annual Dogwood Arts Festival (www.dogwoodarts.com), which takes hold of Knoxville for all of April in a dazzling display of spring blooms. The celebration includes the Chalk Walk, a couple days' worth of street paintings strewn about Market Square; a parade; an all-encompassing arts fair; Bikes and Blooms, a cycle down the dogwood trail; and a host of musical soirees.

Coinciding with the Dogwood Arts Festival is the crazy-popular Rossini Festival (www.knoxvilleopera.com/rossini), a smorgasbord of all things Italian that convenes on and around Gay Street. Sponsored by the Knoxville Opera, the fest includes performances by the professional opera singers as well as shows by the University of Tennessee opera, food vendors, and a street fair.

Held the Sunday before Labor Day, Boomsday (www.boomsday .org) is the biggest party of the year. On top of boasting the largest Labor Day fireworks display in the country, the celebration offers a full lineup of activities throughout the day, which include a Family Fun Zone Area with a petting zoo, rides, food vendors, and more; a karaoke competition; and many performances and boat demonstrations along the waterfront area.

Knoxville knows how to do one thing right, and that's how to throw a party, such as the annual Boomsday celebration the day before Labor Day.
COURTESY OF KNOXVILLE TOURISM & SPORTS CORPORATION

★ ★

The Drop vs. the Dew

While Sun-Drop is Middle Tennessee's liquid crack, East Tennesseans stake claim to Mountain Dew, which had its beginnings with local company Hartman Beverages in the late 1940s. Similar in taste and composition, this lemon-lime concoction originally and fittingly featured a barefoot hillbilly with a rifle and a companion pig as its logo. Today it's much bolder, with a striking green bottling scheme, and tastes remarkably like Sun-Drop. May I suggest a blind taste test?

A Grand Finale

Knoxville

Ask any Knoxvillian who Sergei Rachmaninoff is and, upper echelon of music elitists aside, they probably couldn't tell you. Nevertheless, he is memorialized in an oversize 12-foot-tall bronze version of himself, standing proud and watching over the World's Fair Park.

No, he's not a Tennessean—heck, he's not even American. Sergei was a Russian composer, pianist, and conductor who died in 1943. The statue was created by a Russian sculptor, Victor Bokarev, who was a devout fan of his and wanted to preserve his memory by erecting a monument in the city where the pianist performed his final concert just days before his death. Among other arrangements, concert attendees that day at the University of Tennessee's Alumni Gymnasium were treated to Chopin's Piano Sonata No. 2. After that final performance, Sergei became extremely ill and returned home to Los Angeles to live out his final days. His permanent tribute, *Rachmaninoff: The Last Concert,* is located on the World's Fair Convention Center lawn.

Skunk Apes
LaFollette

Like the (in)famous and mythical jackalope of the Southwest, Tennessee has its own history of a questionable beast—and by questionable I mean, "Is it real or is it fable?" Cryptozoologists (those who study uncataloged animals) swear by the skunk ape's existence; others are not too keen to believe the stories. Whether it's true or not, this hairy primate (allegedly) stands 7 feet tall and weighs in at more than 300 pounds. Sometimes it is mistaken for a Sasquatch or Yeti, which may or may not be the same thing as the skunk ape.

Regardless, there have been a number of sightings that have alerted Tennesseans to its existence, particularly in 2003 in the pinprick town of LaFollette when several people spotted what they thought to be the legendary beast. The cry from townsfolk was so loud, it tipped off nearby researchers at the University of Tennessee, and a whole team of investigators came out to search the area. Skunk apes tend to move in packs, and while many local domesticated animals turned up dead in LaFollette during that time, no photographs, video footage, or concrete evidence materialized to prove the skunk apes' existence.

LaFollette is located 40 miles northwest of Knoxville. Take I-75 North to exit 134, then US 25 West to LaFollette.

Just Like Steve Earle Said
Mountain City

"I learned a thing or two from ol' Charlie, don't you know. You better stay away from Copperhead Road." That's how the famed single "Copperhead Road," written by Steve Earle in the late '80s, concludes. It's a torrid tale of a Vietnam vet who returns to his home of Mountain City, a backwoods little town in Johnson County. Earle wrote of a true place, too, as Copperhead Road is indeed real, only it has since been renamed Copperhead Hollow Road due to a tendency by visitors to steal the sign bearing the name of the famed locale.

★ ★

You can take a trip down memory lane yourself if passing through the area. To reach Copperhead (Hollow) Road, take I-26 East and get off at exit 24, heading east on US 321 toward Elizabethton. Continue to follow the signs for US 321 until you reach Buntontown and see the turnoff for Dry Hill Road. Take it and bear right on Big Dry Run Road, which will turn into Copperhead shortly after.

A People of Intrigue
Newman's Ridge

An enigmatic study in anthropology, the mixed ethnic group called the Melungeons has many a social scientist stumped. They've long been the source of intrigue: As children, many Tennesseans are told they better behave or the Melungeons will come for them. This tribe of sorts is no mythical boogeyman, though; they're very much real. People just don't know many concrete facts about them, hence their air of mystery.

Thought to descend from Spanish or Portuguese explorers, the Melungeons (meaning "mixtures") are a tri-racial group predominantly found along the Cumberland Gap bordering Tennessee and Virginia, with a particular concentration in the town of Newman's Ridge. But it's important to note they're not Anglo, nor are they African or Native American; they are an indigenous people of Appalachia, and it's unknown how long they've inhabited the region.

Back in the first half of the twentieth century, the Melungeons were the focus of many news stories and feature articles, as people were intrigued by this mysterious race; today they are frequently forgotten by their neighbors or too often inaccurately disregarded as "white trash." They were once dismissed and discriminated against because they did not fall into any of America's clearly defined racial categories; they're now a rapidly shrinking breed. You may not even know that you've met one, as many can easily pass for Caucasian these days (centuries ago, they had more of a dark copper skin tone).

Outside of Tennessee, Melungeons are found in Virginia, Kentucky, and North Carolina.

The (Secret) Atomic City
Oak Ridge

This small city that is more or less a suburb of Knoxville is known on an international scale for something other than the mountain culture that infiltrates the region: Oak Ridge lays claim to playing an instrumental role in the development of the atomic bomb, as the city was established in the early 1940s as a base for the Manhattan Project.

Well into World War II, President Franklin Roosevelt decided it was high time to create an atomic bomb, and he needed a way to do so without drawing a lot of attention to the project and the money allocated for it. For the initiative, the U.S. Department of Energy selected four labs and development centers across the country, with Oak Ridge being the first and most important and also the eastern states' hub. The city was selected for the project because of its remote location (distance from seacoasts), accessibility (major highways and railroad routes), small population (it was easy to keep everything quiet), topography (Oak Ridge's valley is 17 miles long), and proximity to Norris Dam (for power resources). Three methods were used to eventually make the atomic bomb, and Oak Ridge played a major part in each one of them.

In order to get the project under way, the federal government invaded the city and a 59,000-acre expanse of land, evicting many of its residents. It wasn't until after the war in 1949 that many were allowed back in to come and go as they pleased, and in 1955 they were finally allowed back onto their own property.

Oak Ridge maintains its science-y reputation to this day, as it is home to the Spallation Neutron Source, which provides the most intense pulsed neutron beams in the world for scientific and industrial research; Oak Ridge National Laboratory, the largest multipurpose lab in the Department of Energy's National Laboratory system; and a whole host of ongoing research projects. It's also been a vital component in many technological discoveries since the war.

To learn more about Oak Ridge's secret past and how it was

kept so hush-hush for so long, visit the American Museum of Science & Energy at 300 South Tulane Ave. For more information, call (865) 576-3200 or visit www.amse.org. There's also the Secret City Commemorative Walk, which travels along East Tennessee Avenue through the original town site of the Manhattan Project. For more information on the walk, call (865) 482-7821.

For Whom the Bell Tolls
Oak Ridge

As a way to remember the Manhattan Project and all those who contributed to it, the Oak Ridge city council installed a memorial in 1992–93, on the fiftieth anniversary of both the city and the project. The International Friendship Bell is meant to serve as an expression of peace between the United States and Japan; it is a traditional Japanese bell incorporating both Asian and American elements that is nearly 7 feet tall and weighs more than two tons.

The bell is one of only twenty or so such structures in the entire world and is located on Badger Avenue in a pavilion in A. K. Bissell Park. For more information, call (800) 877-3429.

Tennessee's Sweetheart
Pigeon Forge

Tennessee is home to many legends, but none have seeped into the hearts of the state's inhabitants quite like Miss Dolly Parton, purveyor of one large voice (and two even larger, um, backup singers). In 1961 the space that would later become her eponymous park opened as a tiny tourist attraction with just a handful of offerings. In 1986 Dolly signed on as co-owner and the park was branded Dollywood (a more appealing name than Silver Dollar City Tennessee, no doubt).

Today Dollywood's 130-acre sprawl is packed all summer long, with the park broken into ten "towns": Dreamland Forest, Adventures in Imagination, Wilderness Pass, Rivertown Junction, Country Fair, the Showstreet, Timber Canyon, Craftsmen's Valley, the Village, and Jukebox Junction. Each holds a plethora of fun, from carnival-style rides to simulators to water flumes. Much of the park's efforts are focused on Southern Appalachian history, and one of its biggest deals is the full-size steam train, which toot-toots its way around the premises. The park is also home to the Southern Gospel Museum and Hall of Fame, as well as a water park, Dollywood's Splash Country. It holds seasonal events every year, such as the Festival of Nations and a Smoky Mountain Christmas.

Dollywood is open from the end of March through the end of December and is located at 2700 Dollywood Parks Blvd. in Pigeon Forge, 35 miles southeast of Knoxville off I-40. For more information, call (800) 365-5996 or visit www.dollywood.com.

Make Like a Ball and Roll

Pigeon Forge

I first decided to hurl myself down a grassy knoll encased in a large transparent globe while in New Zealand. This zany sport invented by the Kiwis is referred to as zorbing and is not for the weak of heart or unadventurous. It can be done solo—in a ball filled with water, so you slip and slide around to avoid injury—or tandem, in which you and your partner are strapped in. You're driven to the top of a hill, helped into your spherical vehicle, and sent rolling. In retrospect, it was a bit like one of those state fair rides that catapults you about the room so many times you fear you may lose the contents of your stomach—but different and fun nonetheless.

Sounds like something you can only find in a country as adventurously wacky as New Zealand, right? Wrong. Imagine my surprise when I returned to Tennessee and found the small town of Pigeon Forge had jumped aboard the zorb bandwagon and was offering a similar experience (and operated by the same company as in New Zealand at that).

But how was it really? you might want to know. Well, let's just say if you're the slightest bit claustrophobic, as I am on occasion, you probably shouldn't let someone zip you up in an airtight case and toss

★ ★

Make like a transparent ball and go catapulting down a grassy knoll in this eccentric activity known as zorbing.

you down a bank. About a third of the way down, I had a borderline panic attack—and hardly anything, except confined spaces, terrifies me—and squeezed my eyes shut for the remainder of the descent, until I rolled to the bottom of the hill and they let me out, to song and dance and much applause. Still, in a word, it was legendary.

Zorb Smoky Mountains is located at 203 Sugar Hollow Rd. in Pigeon Forge, just east of US 441. For more information, call (865) 428-2422 or visit www.zorb.com.

All Hail Dixie
Pigeon Forge

For a peek into Deep South culture, you needn't venture any further than the Dixie Stampede. Another tawdry yet comical local attraction, this dinner theater of sorts is a gold mine of entertainment spanning a hodgepodge of topics; it's no surprise, really, that it's backed by Miss Dolly Parton herself (the woman knows what sells). It's sort of like those Arabian nights or medieval shows you find in every town that relies on tourism, only a bit more authentic given it focuses on the actual region where it takes place.

Prior to dinner and the main event, you'll be treated to an opening act in the Carriage Room, a knee-slapping, foot-stomping bluegrass and country show with a little comedy on the side by in-house band Mountain Rukus. Then you can wander through the stables admiring the palominos, paints, Appaloosas, and quarter horses before finding your table and settling in for a meal. All the while the performers are tickling your senses, you'll be noshing on a four-course meal while soaking in their trick riding, funny animal performances, and your fellow guests participating in such events as a horseshoe competition. Audience members are pitted against each other in a Confederate-Union kind of face-off, and the actual show topics are ever-changing; for example, over Christmas you might find a North vs. South Pole theme with ice skating, sledding, and more. Just don't go in expecting an Emeril Lagasse–worthy meal; the show, not the food, is definitely the emphasis here.

Dixie Stampede Dinner & Show is located at 3849 Parkway in Pigeon Forge. For more information, call (800) 356-1676 or visit www.dixiestampede.com.

★ ★

Mountain Folk
Pikeville

The thing about Tennesseans is that they never try to disguise who they truly are. If this means they wear their hillbilly loud and proud out in the open, then so be it. While the annual Mountaineer Folk Festival is much more than a hillbilly gathering, despite what the name might imply—many regional bluegrass greats have taken the stage here, such as Leroy Troy and Roy Harper—you'll get a good, authentic taste of true mountain life over the weekend.

There's sheep herdin' and shearin', spinnin' and cardin', knittin' and weavin', soap makin', dye makin', doll makin', basket makin'— the whole kit and kaboodle. Additionally, you'll get your share of live demonstrations, from buck dancing to clogging. Homemade candies and cakes and meals of all kinds are doled out generously by the many food vendors on tap.

The Mountaineer Folk Festival takes place at Fall Creek Falls State Park in mid-September each year. To reach the park, take exit 287 off I-40 and follow TN 111 for 40 miles until you reach turnoff signs for the park. For more information, call (423) 881-5298 or visit www.myfallcreekfalls.com.

A Rodent Feast
Pittman Center

When I first heard about Pittman Center on the Travel Channel show *Bizarre Foods with Andrew Zimmern,* I thought surely his account of eating raccoon and opossum meat in the 500-person mountainside town was a tale of fiction. Much to my dismay, I was wrong.

Andrew very much did dine on raccoon brains soaked in barbecue sauce and opossum with a side of taters, both traditional mountain recipes from the region. The foodie also noshed on wasp larvae and squirrel. Lost your appetite yet? If not, do some digging around in Pittman, and you might just be able to enjoy a similar dining experience.

Pittman Center is located 8 miles east of Gatlinburg on US 321.

★ ★

Knifed
Sevierville

Given the state's affinity for firearms, you might expect to find a museum dedicated solely to guns here. Instead, Sevierville keeps things organic with its National Knife Museum, which traces the evolution of the knife from 6,000 BC to the present. Spanning the years in chronological order, more than 12,000 knives create a time line.

The free exhibit is located inside the 88,000-square-foot Smoky Mountain Knifeworks showroom, which has all manners of cutlery, kitchenware, hunting knifes, and pocketknifes available for purchase. There are also specialty hard-to-find items, as well as non-knife merchandise such as martial arts weapons, swords, camping equipment, candles, watches, toys, and Tennessee trinkets.

The National Knife Museum and Smoky Mountain Knifeworks are located at 2320 Winfield Dunn Pkwy. in Sevierville. For more information, call (800) 251-9306 or visit www.smkw.com.

A Walk on the Wild Side
Sevierville

One of the largest reptile zoos in the world is not located in—or even near, for that matter—any rain forest. Rather, it's found in the heart of the Smoky Mountains. With pythons, cobras, and other things that go bump in the night, the indoor Rainforest Adventures Discovery Zoo also showcases furry friends like the ring-tailed lemur, red kangaroo, and crazy-looking coatimundi, and not-so-furry critters like the African crested porcupine. It also houses bugs (cockroaches, scorpions, tarantulas), birds (macaws, cockatoos, parrots), and amphibians (poison dart frogs, American bullfrogs, a number of different toads).

Built by the same people behind Disney's Animal Kingdom, Rainforest Adventures features re-created habitats in an educational and naturalistic setting. The zoo's newest component is the 17,000-square-foot Aussie Walkabout, with all sorts of sheep, wallabies, and other creatures you'd expect to find Down Under.

★ ★

Rainforest Adventures is located at 109 Nascar Dr. in Sevierville. For more information, call (865) 428-4091 or visit www.rfadventures.com.

Gone Fishin'
Sevierville

A charming and quaint man-made pond, well stocked with trout, greets you as you pull into English Mountain Trout Farm & Grill. But don't get too attached to your fishy pals—moments later you'll be baiting your line and casting it into the pond to make one of these swimmers your next meal.

The motto "you hook 'em, we cook 'em" says it all. But should you prefer to watch and not engage in any cruelty to marine life (no one's judging), you can do that, too, and even feed the fish if you like (then order an alternative dish off the menu, like chicken, a burger, or perhaps a salad). All meals are prepared fresh to order, so be ready to settle in for a long and leisurely meal.

English Mountain Trout Farm & Grill is located at 291 Blowing Cave Rd. in Sevierville. For more information, call (865) 429-5553.

Oh, Deer
Sevierville

This petting zoo in the foothills of the Smoky Mountains is an interesting amalgamation of animals you might find on a farm or out in the woods (goats, deer, cows) mingling with animals you wouldn't find in the wild anywhere on this continent (kangaroos, reindeers, zebras, camels). You can feed all the animals and cuddle them as you explore the grounds. Should you want a view from atop, there's also a stable that offers pony and horse rides.

Smoky Mountain Deer Farm & Stables is located at 478 Happy Hollow Lane in Sevierville. For more information, call (865) 428-3337 or visit www.deerfarmzoo.com.

Apples to Apples

Sevierville

On a sprawling sixty-five-acre apple orchard complex, home to 4,000 apple trees, sits a quaint 1920s farmhouse. The farm has been up and running since the early twentieth century, but an aggressive fire burned the original structure to the ground. If you take a wander around the grounds, you'll see the barely visible tracks of the horse-drawn wagons that used to frequent this area.

Given the name and the location, it shouldn't surprise you to learn that every meal begins with fresh apple fritters, apple butter, and the restaurant's signature (nonalcoholic) Applewood Julep. After your meal, take a tour of the complex and learn how such baked goods, candy, wine, and ice cream are made.

Applewood Farmhouse is located at 220 Apple Valley Rd. in Sevierville. For more information, call (865) 429-5700 or visit www.applewood farmhouserestaurant.com.

Get Your Elk Burgers, Hot Off the Grill

Sevierville

There may be nary an elk in this part of the country, but that doesn't stop this '50s-style diner from making it the dish du jour. This shiny, perky establishment specializes in burgers made from animals other than your standard cow, namely elk and bison. The Diner also offers popular Southern delights like fried pickles, fried green tomatoes, hand-dipped shakes, and even malts.

The waitstaff dons poodle skirts and other decade-appropriate attire, and you can play your favorite '50s and '60s tunes on the jukebox. The whole place is decked out in chrome and black-and-white-checkered floors; it's a bit like Johnny Rocket's but with far more authenticity.

The Diner is located at 550 Winfield Dunn Pkwy. in Sevierville. For more information, call (865) 908-1904 or visit www.thediner.biz.

★ ★

Horsin' Around
Soddy-Daisy

With the tagline "ordinary people making extraordinary treasures," you gotta figure that Horsin' Around Carving School is a trove of goodies waiting to be discovered and that its artists are skilled crafts-men. And many of them are, as evidenced by the Coolidge Park Carousel in Chattanooga, an enormous, time-consuming project undertaken by former University of Tennessee art instructor Bud Ellis and a bevy of student carvers. Bud, et. al, spent the better part of twelve years handcrafting and painting the fifty-four animals the carousel's layout called for and even convinced the city to fund the ordeal. Today many a Chattanoogan and visitor alike has enjoyed the fruits of Bud's endeavor.

Many of the people who come to Bud (who has been carving ani-mals for more than twenty years) for instruction do so as a hobby or for help in creating a piece of art they can give to a dear friend or family member or display proudly in their home. Each work generally takes between 300 and 500 hours to complete, using chisels, mallets, drawing knives, and other tools of the trade. While you're hard at work carving a life-size ostrich, you'll likely chat it up with your fel-low classmates as rejuvenating bluegrass fills the air. It's that kind of school, the friendly kind, the kind you can't wait to return to at the end of every class.

But you don't have to be a budding Picasso to study under Bud's tutelage: Non-craftsmen are welcome to enroll in the school, too. Costs are based on what size and structure you aim to create. Horsin' Around Carving School is located at 8316A Dayton Pike in Soddy-Daisy, about 17 miles north of Chattanooga on US 27. For more information, call Bud at (423) 332-1111 or visit www.horsin-around .net.

★ ★

Land of the Lost
Sweetwater

The largest underground lake in the country (and second largest in the world), the Lost Sea was discovered early in the twentieth century when a young boy was playing at the Craighead Caverns and, as little boys are wont to do, decided to crawl down a hole. The cavernous space below the surface was so large, he couldn't see where it started or where it ended. He threw gobs of mud and was met with splashes in response.

It turns out the boy discovered an underground lake with a surface area of more than thirteen acres (the body of water is so large and seemingly never-ending that it's still yet to be fully mapped). Four and a half acres of the area have been designated a Registered Natural Landmark by the National Park Service. Divers and scientists have discovered further rooms and caverns, all flooded with water.

Today you can take boat or spelunking tours—eerie ones at that, as if you're starring in an episode of *The Twilight Zone*—of the below-ground marvel. Not only will you see a glittering display of stalactites and stalagmites, you might even see jaguar tracks from one of the cave's first visitors, dating back some 20,000 years. This very spot was also a meeting place for Cherokee tribes, who held ceremonial rites in the dank space, as well as Civil War soldiers and moonshiners.

The Lost Sea is located at 140 Lost Sea Rd. in Sweetwater, about 7 miles off I-75. For more information, call (423) 337-6616 or visit www.thelostsea.com.

That's a Lot of Paper Clips
Whitwell

In 1998 when a class of eighth-grade students in Whitwell Middle School's Holocaust Education program was trying to fathom how many people died in the Holocaust, they started a project. (Not one of the students was Jewish either, interestingly enough.) They started asking friends and family members for paper clips, every one signifying a victim who died during the extermination of the Jews. The goal was a whopping six million clips—a goal they never actually thought they'd reach.

The project got off to a slow start, but the students stuck with it, creating a Web site and calling on celebrity help. Once it caught the eye of a pair of German journalists who were covering the White House, the project began to gain attention—and momentum. Reporters started showing up in the tiny town of Whitwell (pronounced *whut-wul* by the locals, emphasis on the first syllable), population less than 2,000, profiling the project and writing about the students' endeavors. Soon the likes of Al Gore were writing the children and sending them paper clips, and letters and paper clips from Holocaust survivors and others around the world began pouring in. In the end, the students received more than thirty million paper clips and over 30,000 notes, documents, and artifacts.

The school now houses the Children's Holocaust Museum, containing an authentic German railcar from 1917 filled to the brim with eleven million paper clips: six million representing the murdered Jews, and five million for the other minorities who died during the genocide. German armed forces transported the railcar across the Atlantic on a Norwegian freighter to Baltimore, with its final destination being Whitwell, Tennessee. Eleven million additional paper clips in the form of a monument memorialize the children of Terezin. Guided tours are given by appointment on Friday mornings.

A documentary about the project, *Paper Clips,* was released in 2004, and the students who participated have become legends of sorts. Whitwell Middle School is located at 1 Butterfly Lane in Whitwell, about 24 miles northwest of Chattanooga off TN 28. For more information, call (423) 658-5635.

index

index

index

index

index